Every Day Is a Gift

Other books by Mary Ellen Ostrander

Puff, the Sea Lion: A Love Story

To both of my Fathers in Heaven:
The Lord Almighty
and the gifts He gave to me,
my father on earth,
Thomas Blazynski,
who taught me by example
how to be gentle to all and to love animals;
and to my mother Darylann Blazynski,
who showed me to never give up and to trust in the
Lord.

Table of Contents

Preface

I have been fortunate in my life to have loved greatly. I have been given a wonderful human family to share my journey with. We are an unconventional family because we do not share the same blood. We are all connected through marriage or adoption, from my parents and siblings to my husband and children. We each have different human parents and genetics. I am amazed when I look around our family table. Our love is abundant and it is not some coincidence. I feel there is tremendous power in our love, one created by God. Every day we have a chance to love and receive love. It is our choice each moment each day.

This love includes all of the animals in my life, from my dogs and cats at home to the numerous animals I have cared for during my many years as a zookeeper. I started young; I was still in my teens, learning about exotic animal care of many different varieties from axolotls to elephants, from apes to zebras. This story, however, focuses on a special group of California sea lions at a zoo in New York State. Yes, I am still a zookeeper, albeit not so young anymore. This memoir reflects my unique experiences and perspectives; therefore, I've been purposefully vague about certain places and specific people. I am compelled to tell you about the loves in my life. If I do not share with you the beauty that their lives have brought to me, I would be doing them and you a great disservice.

Caring for animals at the zoo became my profession, my vocation, my life's work. I discovered early on that each animal has a discrete personality—no two are alike—and they have individual needs, very much like each person is an individual with different genetics and life experiences that makes them who they are. If you take the time to observe animals and their behavior, you discover so much. I want people to understand this and I hope as many

1

people as possible will think of animals as the jewels they are on this earth.

In my first book, *Puff the Sea Lion; A Love Story*, I wrote about my love for Puff and Flounder, two California sea lions that lived at the zoo where I work. Without intention, Puff became the "animal child" of my heart. My love for him was above all others. I never planned for that to happen; he just innocently snuck in there.

For those unfamiliar with California sea lions, these marine mammals eat fish and mainly live on and off the beaches of California. They are super soft and fuzzy when they are dry and slick and silky when wet. I know this because I have been lucky enough to pet, even hug, the sea lions in my care. They remind me of aquatic Labrador retrievers. With their big chocolate pools for eyes, heart-shaped noses, tiny ears, flippers instead of paws, and playful demeanor, they will captivate you. These animals became my sweet pinniped family. As their teacher/trainer I taught them to trust humans and our actions through positive reinforcement training. Simply put, I feed them their daily fish when they are behaving in a way I would like them to offer again, such as allowing me to touch them, patiently waiting for their turn, or having them sit still while something they might find scary is happening, like a door shutting or a peer barking. Feeding and playing with them every day has created the trusting bond that I call love.

"The Rocky Coasts" is the area of our zoo, built in 1997, where the California sea lions and polar bears have their habitats. In an indoor, heated, underground gallery, there are graphics to educate the public about California sea lions and polar bears as well as large windows to observe the animals displaying natural behavior throughout the day, year-round. If you are lucky enough to experience it, the sea lions will actually play with you at these windows. At the time of this story, the zookeepers who worked in

2

this area also shared in the care of two Sandhill cranes, two female Amur tigers, thirty-six African black-footed penguins, two gray wolves, two Canada lynx, a salt-water coral reef tank, a snowy owl, one female polar bear, and four California sea lions.

This story begins after Flounder's death in 2013 from kidney failure. As a recap for any of you who may be unacquainted with my first book, I had watched his birth in the summer of 1991; at ten o'clock in the morning on June 21 of that year Flounder came into this world. To be with an animal at both the first moment of his life and during his last hours moved me profoundly. Life is precious and every moment is a gift to cherish. I once read that grief is our last expression of love. We are never ready for the pain that a loss may bring us and I am confident we never will be. It is how we handle the emptiness that counts. Now, when I grieve greatly, I understand that I feel this way because I have loved greatly. This understanding comforts me during life's many trials.

Flounder and I went on a journey together that included many other travelers. My heart is full of beautiful memories of Flounder. I loved Flounder—what a treasure he was! We celebrated his life every day we shared together. I will always be grateful to God for the many years I had with him. He was playful, patient, and understanding as he allowed me to teach him during my early years as a sea lion trainer. I was exuberant and ignorant, but always had good intentions. Together the two of us learned about the power of positive reinforcement training and relationship building.

Flounder taught me along with at least a dozen other budding zookeepers the correct way to train sea lions with compassion and understanding. Animals do not need to be dominated. They need a friend, an advocate to teach them with gentleness and love. How do I know this? Every animal that I have taught throughout my career has proved this to me over and over again by learning each of the behaviors I was teaching them with ease, proving that they had learned to trust me. They trusted me because I was kind and gentle with them and understood the principles of positive reinforcement and used this tool each and every time I was with them.

Puff was born in 2006 and arrived at our zoo as a ten-month old pup in 2007. Flounder was his only sea lion playmate. Soon Puff and I embarked on a journey that led to an unbreakable bond. It shook me to my core when he passed away unexpectedly on October 4, 2012 at the young age of six. After Puff's death, friends reminded me that it happened on the Feast of Saint Francis, who in the Catholic Church is the patron saint of animals and nature. I know it was not a coincidence that Puff passed on this feast day. Francis is the name I chose for my middle name when I was twelve years old, for my Confirmation, which is a Catholic sacrament. I've always had a fascination for animals. I could never have imagined the plan God had for me or the voyage that this love would take me on. Puff's life and death brought me closer to God. If I had never loved Puff, I would not have written my first book which was a testament to my belief and faith in God. I am absolutely certain that God had blessed me with this gift to understand more about unconditional love than I had before, and for that, I am eternally grateful.

Although every day I struggled to get by, I never questioned God. All animals belong to Him first and I was lucky enough to love my animal friends for as long as God sees fit. I was devastated nonetheless. To some people, they were our zoo's ambassadors for their species in the wild, for others, fun animals to learn from, but they were family to me. During the thirty-four years that I have been a zookeeper, I have spent many holidays and weekends with the sea lions and other animals in my care. Every zoo is a 24/7 operation. Zookeepers are essential personnel who are needed each and every day to keep the animals safe and the zoo secure. On an average snowy day or during a blizzard, I shovel snow and salt

4

the paths of the sea lions' beach numerous times throughout the day to ensure they can exit the water with ease. (I also shovel paths for the zoo guests who are adventurous enough to visit our zoo on a snowy day). On 90-degree days, I provide the sea lions with ice blocks that I prepare ahead of time and turn on hoses for them to play with the water and swim through the spray. It is a perfect way for them to cool down and have fun on a hot summer's day. I also set up misters for each of the other animals I care for (the visitors appreciate it as well, especially the young children). I am by the animals' sides if they are ill or even on days when I am ill myself. I think about the animals in my care both when I am at work and when I am not. They are constantly in my prayers. They are very close family to me.

Years ago, before I became a mother, a docent smiled and said to me, "You are just like their mother." I smiled back but was silently thinking the lady was a bit "off." However, consider this: if you are a thorough and conscientious zookeeper, you feed the animals in your care only the healthiest, hand-selected and best quality of food and you assure that they have clean water. You make sure they have safe things with which to play every day; that their beds are fresh and clean; that they have access to quality shelter in inclement weather; that they are safe. It is essential they are treated with love and compassion every time you are with them, not only so they learn the husbandry behaviors we need them to acquire, but that they also learn how to trust humans and their actions. I only came to realize this many years later—that docent knew exactly what she was talking about. Good mothers do all these things and more. You don't have to give birth to someone to take on the role of a mother.

While I was at work one morning several months after Puff and Flounder had passed away, I was thinking about my manuscript and the love I had for Puff and Flounder. I asked the Lord what the next steps in my life should be. I asked for guidance and peace. I was walking towards the underwater viewing area to observe and play with Star and Angel. I noticed a docent (an educator) in the gallery. I had met her before, but we had only spoken briefly with each other. Her name is Maureen. We talked about Flounder and Puff and how wonderful they were. We shared stories of all their antics at the gallery glass. I told Maureen many of the different stories of taking care of them and loving them. We grieved together.

Working in my own little world with the sea lions, I didn't realize how attached other people who were not their caregivers actually were to them. I was beginning to understand that these beautiful animals meant a great deal to many other people. When Puff and Flounder died, our zoo received sympathy cards written by children with crayon drawings of Puff and Flounder. At times, a parent would do the writing and a very small child drew tears and hearts around a black oval with eyes. Visitors, volunteers, and docents would just come up to me sobbing and hug me and then we would babble and cry together; our love for these two sea lions brought strangers together through a shared loss. In a strange way, it felt good that Puff and Flounder were greatly appreciated when they were alive and dearly missed now that they were gone.

Maureen asked me if she could interview me for a book she was working on about our zoo's history. I said, "Absolutely." Shortly thereafter we sat down for the interview; I told Maureen many stories particularly about the sea lions and the adventures in which they included me. I mentioned that I had just finished writing a story about them. Somehow this revelation led to Maureen reading the manuscript (then her agreeing to edit it!). Needless to say, over the next year, during the editing process, we became very close. Maureen is now one of my closest and dearest friends.

Maureen took me to a local author workshop at our central public library where I learned how to self-publish my book. It was suggested authors established their own publishing company. I took that advice and opened my own business which I named The Lewis Sebastian Press. My company's title and trademark are named after Lou, our spotted hyena at the zoo; Lou found a place in my heart from the moment I met him. At the library event, we were also advised to hire a graphic designer for the cover of our book. So, like any other novice author would do, I immediately began a search for a graphic designer on the Internet. I chose one young lady because of her style, and also by an overwhelming feeling that I had to select her. Amazingly, when I contacted her, out of all the graphic designers in the nation, this one designer, the one that stood out to me, just so happened to live a quarter of a mile from Maureen; Maureen lives a quarter of a mile from my mother. God was making this very easy for me! I immediately began spending time with the graphic designer, creating the book's cover, then I would head over to Maureen's house for an editing session, and then I would go to Mom's for a chat. I will be forever grateful for such loving support during the time of the book's editing. For readers who think this may have been simply a coincidence, I am positive it was not. My prayers had been answered in a way that I had never considered asking for. Again, this could not be simply a coincidence. God knows me better than anyone and He loves all of us unconditionally. We only need to love Him back.

I am compelled again to share my adventures with you. My mind and soul will not allow me to rest until I share with you the blessings that were bestowed upon me by God in the shape of California sea lions, Star and Angel. My story begins with their arrival at our zoo and in my heart. I hope you get to know them, cheer their victories, and cry with me at their losses. Please enjoy my story.

Chapter 1
California Girls

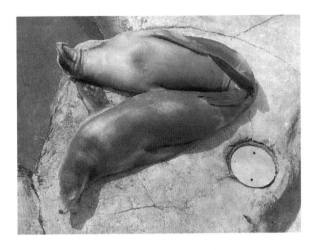

Star on her back and Angel by her side—beach buddies

When Star and Angel arrived at our zoo in January 2011, each of these beautiful little sea lions was eighteen months old and weighed 110 pounds. They were rescued on the California coast. Angel was found on December 4 and Star on December 5, 2009. Already there was something connecting me to them, as if we were meant to be together. I do not believe in coincidences; December 5 holds a special place in my heart because it is my mother's birthday.

Veterinarians at the rescue center in California deemed Angel and Star non-releasable due to the gunshot wounds they had sustained. Star's left eye had to be removed due to trauma caused by one of the bullets. The x-rays that were sent along with her showed shrapnel pieces remained in her head. Angel had wounds to her right flipper which abscessed. She hobbles on land now. I know it's hard to comprehend, but, yes, it is illegal to shoot California sea lions and yes, nevertheless, humans shot them.

When Star and Angel arrived at the zoo, they feared humans. I am certain they did not understand that their rescuers were helping them as they removed the bullets, administered medicine, and tubed food into their stomachs. But they were fighters—they survived. After getting a clean bill of health from the veterinarians at the marine mammal rescue center, Star and Angel were crated, loaded onto a plane, and flown thousands of miles where they arrived safely at the zoo.

I have been working with animals for years and it never once occurred to me that sea lions were being shot. I understand that most animal species have been shot by humans at one time or another, so why should I be surprised? I just had never actually met a sea lion that had survived such trauma, let alone have them placed in my care. Looking at their small, injured bodies gave me a surge of love similar to when I held my children for the first time or brought a homeless dog into our house. I was determined to make sure that the rest of their lives would be healthy, safe, and fun.

Our primary objective was getting them to trust humans after so many negative things had happened to them at such a young age. I knew they were afraid because they'd retreat at our presence. Unlike all the other animals I cared for, who have been trained to come when their names are called, initially Angel and Star would slide away from us as soon as anyone entered the room. Animals have a freeze, flight or fight instinct. They need plenty of room to flee any area when they feel unsafe. I did not want to accidentally scare Star and Angel into thinking they had to protect themselves.

Studies show that positive reinforcement training is the most effective and humane training method. In the last thirty years zoos have changed for the better. True zoo professionals are gaining knowledge on the physical and mental needs of the animals in our care and are striving daily to improve their lives. I have been there to witness and help in the progress. In my many years of animal training, I have written, spoken about, and given various presentations on the power of positive reinforcement and the relationships that are built through trust and respect between humans and many other species of animals. It's the method we use at this zoo.

First, Angel and Star needed to accept food from us, learning to associate fish with their name. They soon began to understand that we brought fish in the buckets we carried. To ensure name recognition, we would say their names as each gobbled up the fish. In time, their name meant a delicious fish to them. This was step one in building a relationship with them. Some trainers go no further than achieving name recognition. We wanted to teach Star and Angel more. Training is teaching. Animals learn from training and in turn I learned from Star and Angel. Both, in their own way, taught me to be patient and to do things on their time. It was only when they felt safe and relaxed that we would and could move forward.

Over the next few years, these two "California girls" learned many husbandry behaviors such as getting on a scale to be weighed, holding still for x-rays and ultra sound, voluntarily receiving an injection and eye drops, accepting an anal thermometer, and entering and leaving the holding area when we asked. Positive reinforcement training was knitting a connection between us. Eventually they each let me touch every part of their body; done on their time it took a few years, but they would allow me and my colleagues to give them a full body exam any day at any time. We were forging a lifelong bond of trust and understanding.

Angel was shy and fearful. When training Angel, I learned to be calm and precise because she learned best this way. I would sit next to her, petting her and calling her "my sweet baby," slowly feeding her fish, rubbing her back, chest and face. She would relax and her shiny black eyes would reflect my face. When Angel was uncomfortable with her surroundings, she would open her mouth wide and her eyes would widen with worry. If she was very uncomfortable, she would retreat to a place where she felt safer, her mouth still open. Desensitizing her to different people, objects, and activities was one of my goals to give her a better quality of life. To this day she has never bitten a trainer or visitor to her habitat. I would like to say it was because of the excellent training she had, but I know it has a lot to do with her sweet and gentle demeanor. Her name suits her. She has great patience with the humans in her life and I love her for this quality. She decided we were worth her trust. This was quite a gift from her; one I do not take for granted.

One snowy wintry day I brought a special-needs young man to visit Angel and Star. He was so excited. We stepped outside to the sea lion habitat. The day was clear and bright and I shared his anticipation. I love showing others how wonderful the animals I care for are; I want everyone to appreciate their uniqueness, beauty, and intelligence. When we approached them, Star and Angel hopped up on the beach to get a better look at their newest visitor. Her curiosity satisfied, Star dove back into the water, but Angel stayed a little longer, I was happy to see this because Angel was the warier of the two. Then she did the strangest thing; she looked up and opened her mouth like she does when she feels unsafe. As I stepped back to look up too, Angel dove into the pool at the precise moment a small avalanche of snow slid off the sea lion overlook and landed on our visitor's head. The snow covered his eyes for a moment and slid down the back of his coat. We were totally surprised. He looked at me with a big smile on his face and we broke out in laughter. You never know what will happen when you work at a zoo, especially when you are a guest at the sea lions' beach.

Every Day Is a Gift

Star was quick in body and mind. I would call her inside for her daily exam and training session and after our "business" was accomplished, we would have some fun. Some trainers call this a secondary reinforcer. A secondary reinforcer is something an animal looks forward to that is not a necessity to live like food or water. It is something you can pair with food or it could be "playtime." Food and fun were important, but it was really our relationship that Star and I enjoyed and looked forward to throughout the day. I would sing to her and she would "light-up" with excitement and then begin to make up her own routines. She liked it when I sang "go bananas, go-go bananas." She also liked the song "Starfish, Starfish, what about Starfish?" Unconventional by some training standards, perhaps, but we liked being silly together. I would keep singing and she would make up a string of behaviors. She would link previously learned behaviors together on her own accord during my song. Like a windup toy wound just a little too tight, she would slide from room to room, dunk her head in the water, and spin around. I would laugh and hug her. Then as I continued the song, she would invent something new like putting her face in the running hose stream. I would say: "You're silly; do it again," and she would! We called that behavior "put your face in the water" (how original). Star taught herself behaviors, I named them, and she would remember what I named them.

One day a mosquito landed on Star's head during a training session. Like any of us would do, without thinking, I slapped the mosquito and her head too in the process. She did not flinch. At that moment, I knew how much she trusted me. I gave her a dream's worth of fish after the unexpected contact. I hoped this reinforced her acceptance of my foolish error. Could you imagine that a young, wild California sea lion would have this intelligence and personality and put such trust in a human being? It took my breath away. Discovering such things is one of the reasons I wanted to share her story.

Star was in charge when it came to our young bull sea lion, Puff. In 2011 when Star arrived, she was a busy pup, full of energy and Puff, who also enjoyed playing, found her extremely attractive. From the moment they were first introduced, Puff could not get enough of her! Often she would take his toys and play "keep-away." I recall fondly (and this is my favorite story) one time when Puff and Star were playing with a doorstop. We used this doorstop to hold a door open inside the sea lion holding room. I would often find that doorstop missing. Since he had been trained to fetch, I would ask Puff to dash outside and get it for me. One day while I was walking by the underwater viewing windows in the public gallery, I saw Star zipping through the water with that wooden doorstop in her mouth. Speeding right behind her was Puff. She had the prize among prizes, but I knew right away that he would never be able to catch that little imp. Obviously, they were enjoying each other and having the time of their lives, or at least Star was.

They played and had fun with each other until the day Puff passed away at the young age of six on October 4, 2012. I lost a piece of my heart that day. I am sure Star mourned as much as I, but she had a distraction I did not. Star was pregnant. On June 1, 2013, Star gave birth to a healthy pup, Puff's son. Her pregnancy was not apparent to any of us because she gained only a few pounds during the gestation period. She was just a pup herself, considering she was only three years old when she conceived.

Female California sea lions continue to increase their internal layers of blubber until they are eight years old. Therefore, they are not considered fully grown until then. We always gave Star all the fish she could eat and she always had a good appetite. Star continued to eat and was playful until the day before she gave birth. When I left work that evening, Star looked uncomfortable on the beach and answered with a little groan when I said good night to her. For a moment, I wondered if she was about to give birth. It was June, the birthing season for sea lions. It was possible; Puff had been an intact male, but she was so young.

The loss of Puff and Flounder in the past few months had clouded my thoughts. I was living day to day trying to get through the pain from their loss. I wouldn't allow myself to consider the possibility of a sea lion pup. The next day, June 1, 2013, I had the day off from work. I was in my backyard with my son when my supervisor phoned me and said, "PUFF DID IT!" I hadn't heard his name in a long time and hearing it hurt and felt good at the same time. I asked her to repeat what she said. She told me that Star had a pup! Immediately I jumped into my car and raced to the zoo to witness this little miracle. On that incredible morning, when a colleague of mine first checked on Star, she was in the sea lion holding area by herself. This was unusual; normally she would not be found resting indoors alone. She preferred to rest outside with the other sea lions. Less than an hour later, when he returned to feed Star, he saw blood on the floor and a beautiful pup!

When the pup was only a few days old he (we were pretty sure it was male because I saw it urinate) fell asleep on his back in the sea lion holding room. He was tiny, helpless, adorable, and fiercely guarded by his mother almost every second. While he slept, Star took the opportunity to go for a swim, leaving her napping pup unattended. At the same moment, my supervisor and I crept in, approached the pup and confirmed that the pup was indeed male. My colleague who first discovered the newborn pup suggested that since he was the person who first discovered the pup, he should be the one to name him. We all agreed. He chose the name "PJ", meaning Puff Junior. We smiled as we looked at "Puff Junior" and then smiled again at each other as we quietly exited without ever being noticed by Star or her newborn pup.

Chapter 2
Playtime Is Learning Time

PJ at one-month old

When Puff died, I was inconsolable. I wanted to care less, but because he meant so much to me the grief was overwhelming. Then God in His glorious way gave me a way back—watching Star care for her pup for the very first time. At just a few days old, PJ would jump into the inside pool. Quickly Star would dive in, grab him by the scruff of his neck, toss him out of the water, and "yell" at him. He was just a newborn, but she was communicating with him all the time and he began to understand.

Every Day Is a Gift

When he was four days old, PJ got the surprise of his short life. He was minding his own business, resting quietly indoors, being a cute pup. Star, just turning four years old and still a youngster herself, decided she wanted to see if this little sea lion could swim. I could tell by observing her in the inside holding room. She looked outside through the door to the large pool and then glanced down at PJ. She looked out the doors again and down at PJ once more. I thought to myself, "It looks to me like she has a plan to take PJ outside." Sure enough, she picked him up by the scruff with her teeth, carried him outside, went up a small embankment, and tossed him in the water. I was confident in my swimming ability, knowing that if she needed help I was fully capable of rescuing PJ if needed. I also was sure Star would not like me jumping in the water with her beloved pup, but I was ready to risk her wrath. I had a net nearby as well in case both Star and I could not get PJ out of the water. Wild sea lions are introduced into the oceans at this age, like PJ, and are not good swimmers until they are a month old.

The outdoor pool holds about 110,000 gallons of water and the filtration system processes it at about 100,000 gallons an hour. As I watched, I thought "boy he swims poorly." I looked at Star and couldn't help but smile because she had the same expression on her face. That one-eyed, first-time sea lion mother dove in the pool, picked PJ up by the scruff, unceremoniously tossed him out of that large pool over the embankment, and then vocalized sounds telling him to go back inside. He looked bewildered, but he slowly made his way indoors. After that demonstration of exceptional motherly decision-making, going forward we gave Star the chance to make all decisions pertaining to her pup. Even though the doors to go in and out of the sea lion exhibit were opened at all times, Star would not let PJ go outside again for almost a month. She thought he was inept at swimming and was correct.

16

Initially, Star only allowed me to watch her activities with PJ from approximately 12 feet away. If I got any closer, her mothering instinct kicked in and she gave me "the look." I knew what that look meant. She did not have to warn me with any other actions. I understood. I have been working with animals for many years. Her pup came before me now and I was proud of her for protecting him.

Star taught PJ to follow her inside to their holding area. She was very vocal, communicating with him in different sounding barks. In one instance, Star stood in front of PJ, moved a few inches away from him, vocalized, and then turned to look at him. He moved forward. This would go on for about ten minutes. When his attention span was too short and he turned and started going the other way, Star's vocals would go to a higher pitch. It was quite apparent this was a mother-son training session. She had a plan, a teaching agenda. I wondered, as I listened to their "conversation" (she was so chatty with her pup, almost constantly making noises), if she was imitating me because whenever I taught her, I was always making noises, talking away during training like she was now. Now she had become the teacher; PJ was her student. Star allowed me to watch these lessons. In those early weeks he learned, among other things, to follow Star inside, to swim, and to haul himself out of the inside pool.

The door to the outside pool was left open during the day. As Star began to trust PJ on his own she would leave him from time to time to swim outside with Angel. On occasion, while swimming by the open door she would call inside to PJ. If he did not bleat back in response she would be inside in a flash, moving her head back and forth, berating him. Oh, we all knew what she was saying, "Answer me, young man." I felt bad for him because often he was trying to nap. He would groggily lift his head and give her a little noise and usually that would appease Star. If not, Star would slide into the holding room bark-honking, demanding his reply. If I was in the inside holding room with him and he didn't answer I would say, "Oh, you better answer or you are in trouble," then I would step out of the area so when Star came in concerned, she did not blame it on my presence.

For seven days Star would not let Angel come inside to see the pup. Angel was very upset by this, because she usually slept with Star. They had been best friends since their rescue two years previously. I could tell Angel was upset by her swimming behavior. In the week since PJ was born, Angel had been swimming continuously in the outside pool. Angel was getting water logged; her flippers looked whitish at the tip. It is similar to what happens to people when they have been in the bathtub too long; our fingers and toes get pruney. You would think this would not happen to a marine mammal that lives in water most of the time, but it did. She came out of the water only to eat and get examined; she would eat quickly and go right back to swimming. I couldn't console her; try as I might, she wanted Star.

As a new mom, Star was instinctively very protective of PJ. We were proud of every choice Star made. PJ was thriving! Then came the day when the planets must have been aligned right, because Star decided to allow the "prisoner" sea lion pup to go outside. Star was so hesitant to let PJ go in the water, visitors, docents, volunteers, and some of the zoo staff began to think PJ would be the only terrestrial sea lion in existence. They were wrong, of course, and delighted to see this little newcomer when he made his independent swimming debut almost four weeks to the day after his mom first tossed him into the water. After teaching him to swim, Star taught PJ where to hide and how to follow her everywhere.

One day, one of the vet staff was on rounds at the sea lion habitat and said that he did not see the sea lion pup. There were five trained zoo staff in the area at the time; we immediately reacted and entered the sea lion beach in search of PJ. First, I observed Star's behavior. She was swimming about leisurely. If anything was wrong with PJ, I was quite certain she would *not* be calm. A few of the sea lion trainers were searching the sea lion beach from every angle. He had to be here somewhere. We checked the filter intakes because the suction on the filter system grates is powerful. Again, if PJ was struggling I knew Star would not be relaxed. She knew where he was; we just had to find him. One staff member went down on his knees to lie on his stomach so he could look under some rock work where one of the pool's skimmer baskets was esthetically camouflaged to look like a little cave. That staff member had to move fast after he got a glimpse of PJ because Star was there in an instant to protect her precious pup. She meant business and my coworker retreated. For the next month or so, we knew where to find PJ.

I read later that sea lions naturally teach their pups to hide when they go out hunting for fish. How did Star know this? Before she was shot, did Star remember her mother teaching her in the oceans of California? Considering the possibility that she did remember her past made me want to protect her even more. Now look at her guarding her pup! Watching this new mother's confidence and competence grow thrilled me.

Just like a human child does, PJ began to learn his name; we'd say it whenever we were near him pointedly looking at him while we spoke. When we stood above the "cave" and said his name, most times he would peek out. At times, I watched Star swim over to the cave with one of the small plastic watering cans she enjoyed playing with in her mouth and deposit it in the cave for PJ to play with. I had to wonder if sea lions that live in the ocean give their pups something to play with when they leave them to hunt. Or was this just my Starfish being her brilliant self, doing something totally unique because she saw a need and found a solution? What a pleasure to watch!

Every Day Is a Gift

Now that PJ was outside occasionally, Angel had the opportunity to approach him. Watching through my tears of joy and relief as Star finally allowed Angel to get close to her pup, I saw Angel sniff PJ in greeting, her whiskers flexing forward towards him questioningly. Nevertheless, Star watched very closely to see what Angel would do. Star didn't allow the interaction to last very long before she barked-lunged at Angel to get her to go back into the water away from her pup.

PJ was less than a month old when I saw Angel lying on the beach holding her stomach with her flippers and breathing with her mouth open. She was obviously very uncomfortable with abdominal distress. She came into the inside holding area to separate herself from Star and PJ. I reported her behavior to the vet staff and was asked to keep observing her. Did Puff breed Angel as well? How exciting if this were true; PJ would have a playmate. It looked to me like she was in labor. I remained after my scheduled work hours watching and waiting with high anticipation. Angel was by herself with me close at hand. After several hours, she began swimming and when I offered her some fish she ate them. I had heard of false pregnancy in marine mammals but not false labor. The sea lions are always teaching me something new.

We decided to do some tests. Angel is trained to allow us to x-ray her and ultrasound her. These tests were inconclusive, however; fortunately, the vet staff did not see a mass, but neither did they see a pup. Angel was back to her old self in no time and PJ became very interested in playing with her. Although Star didn't like this at first, she soon discovered that having a built-in babysitter was a very good thing.

I saw Star was getting tired of the 24/7 routine many of us as new parents know. One day Star wanted to nap on the beach, her eye lids were closing then opening slowly. I knew this feeling all too well from the time when I was up with my own children during the night. Angel proved to be the best friend that Star may have forgotten she had had since meeting at the sea lion rescue in California only three years prior. I recall one particular occasion when Angel was indeed a great friend when Star really needed one.

Star was trying to sleep on the rocky beach of her home when PJ, the equivalent of a sea lion toddler, repeatedly leaped out of the pool and bounced on top of his very tired mother. Star appeared too exhausted to protest. I knew the feeling from when my own children wanted to play when I was tired and trying unsuccessfully to sleep. I felt bad for Star. PJ had an abundance of items to play with, but nothing is like mom. I was about to find him a new toy, hose, or chunk of ice to play with, hoping that it would distract PJ from his sleepy mother when Angel came to Star's rescue. Angel gently approached the feisty, leaping PJ. It looked to me as if she was trying to get his attention in her quiet way. She swam close to PJ and tried to make eye contact.

Angel didn't make a sound. I have only heard her vocalize once, when she was a pup calling us for food. At the time, I didn't realize why Angel was vocalizing. Years later I understood that that was why she was calling at the door when the zookeepers entered. It was so different from Star, because when Star began calling me for food she made it very clear to me that that was what she was doing. Star could see me walking by her outdoor habitat as I checked on her throughout the day. If she was hungry, she would make direct eye contact with me and bark-honk, then dash inside and wait by the door I entered when I fed her. I'd see her peeking through the crack between the double doors with her only eye, eager for my arrival. Star vocalized enough for everyone whether calling to me when I walked by her habitat or giving directions to her pup. She always had a vocal opinion and I would not have changed her one bit! Star's personality brought a lot of energy to this sea lion family.

Every Day Is a Gift

Angel, quiet as usual, tried using eye contact to lure PJ away from his exhausted mother, but it did not work. It was very interesting to watch Angel's thought wheels turn. The next time PJ jumped off his mother and went back in the pool Angel positioned herself between him and the land so that she was in between PJ and Star. Angel looked at PJ and slightly moved her head back and forth in a playful gesture. I have only seen sea lion pups gesture this way to elicit play. Angel was speaking "pup" to PJ. PJ looked up at the sleeping Star ready to leap on her again, but Angel shook her head gently never breaking eye contact with PJ and began to slowly swim backwards. PJ was wound up in play and didn't seem to even notice Angel. He looked at Angel and his body language said, "That is not interesting." Before he could bounce on his mother again, Angel porpoised straight up out of the water. Now that got PJ's attention; he went right after Angel with his mouth open in a playful posture of aggression. Instead of Angel opening her mouth back at PJ, to tell him to stop —that this was not appropriate behavior—she bent her head backward towards her tail and began spinning under water. It looked like PJ wanted to wrestle, so Angel spun under water again; he closed his mouth and copied Angel. He copied her spins and attempted her beautiful porpoising. His chubby little body could not do what Angel's could, but that didn't matter; he was having fun. Star was sleeping and that was the goal. Success! Thanks Angel!

After a few minutes of this diversion PJ swam away to play by himself like many children do. Now tell me this: what reason besides being a very good friend would lead Angel to go out of her way to entertain Star's pup? Angel had nothing to gain when she occupied PJ. Showing great empathy, she went out of her way to help a friend. The more we observe animals the more we can learn. We only need to take the time. Every time they showed me their compassion for each other my love for them grew.

Sea lion pups drink their mothers' milk until they are about a year old. Star would call PJ to her when she wanted him to come and nurse. Zoo visitors commented on this natural activity and spoke to their children about mammals, including humans, drinking mother's milk. PJ would also tell Star when he was hungry and they would choose a spot to nurse. I recall they engaged in a lot of vocalizing and nursing that summer. It was a nursing extravaganza; he was nursing constantly. When California sea lions are born, they weigh on average fifteen pounds. When PJ was seven months old he weighed 82 pounds; he was a little butterball. People would comment on how "juicy" he looked. I do not believe they said it to be cruel, but because he really did look like a succulent tidbit; he was adorably chunky and fuzzy. He had the sweetest innocent face on that delicious body. The expression on his face told the zoo staff and guests that he had very little fear with a mother like Star watching over him and his education was in an extremely safe environment. If he lived in the ocean, you could only imagine what a Killer Whale or Great White shark would think if PJ floated by.

I had a lot of fun watching PJ and the other sea lions play. Thinking of new toys to give them to elicit natural behaviors, watching them play together, or seeing them solve a food puzzle, gave the sea lions and me many moments of joy. One afternoon Star and Angel were sleeping on the beach. PJ was swimming around quietly and I thought "he is being such a good pup because he's leaving Star and Angel to rest by themselves; he needs a new toy." I remembered how his father loved pinecones. Around the sea lion habitat there is an abundance of pine trees and lucky for us, pinecones. I gathered five rather large ones and, unnoticed by PJ, added them to the outside pool. Very soon PJ found the new playthings and began pushing them through the water, one after another, with his nose, mouth, chin and front flippers, over and under and sideways, in as many ways as mathematically possible.

He enjoyed the pinecones for the entire afternoon, dispersing them to different parts of the pool, twirling them through the water, his chubby body spinning this way and that, somersaulting with them, holding them under his flippers, inventing new games as he went along. He reminded me so much of my own children when they were very young, using their imaginations when they found a similar treasure when we were out hiking or in our own backyard and play with it for hours.

One day our zoo received a shipment of long-handled, hand-held scrub brushes. I "borrowed" one for PJ. I watched as he attempted to push the bristles along the glass underwater. The zoo guests and I were captivated watching him discover what he could do with this new plaything. I told them he was my habitat-cleaning apprentice as I watched him move the brush up and down on the glass directly in front of a throng of visitors. Parents understood my joke having their own young human helpers like this at home and we laughed together. I took pictures and videos of him pushing the brush along the outside pool floor. Sometimes the bristles would be up and not down (the way they should be for the purpose of scrubbing). I commented with a giggle, "He's new at the job." Again, guests laughed at my joke and at his playfulness. I understood he was learning about his environment through touch, just as we humans do.

Part of the sea lion beach is a large dirt area we made into a flower garden. I have planted many flowers in this garden, some as memorials to the animals I have loved who have passed away. Each is represented by a different variety of flower.

The black-eyed susans remind me of Nikita and Dimitri, the Amur leopards I cared for years ago. The black middle of the flowers represents their spots and the gold petals are similar to their beautiful golden color. The abundance of the flowers signifies the many times I would visit them and how much I loved them. I can still hear them calling to me as I approached them. Dimitri's vocalization brings a warm feeling to me as I remember him "saying" as I hurried to his habitat, "WOW. WOW. WOW," as he scrambled in his excitement to meet me. He would push his head hard on the mesh while rubbing it in greeting. His blatant affection stole my heart (I feel a burst of love right now as I write this) and I will never forget him. Nikita, his sister lived adjacent to Dimitri. They were not housed together because they were related and in nature Amur leopards live solitary lives with the exception of mothers and cubs. Nikita would flop on her back and hold her back paws with her front paws at my approach and purr loud enough for our zoo guests to hear. She was obviously glad to see me as I told her what a "good girl" she was, that I loved her and those crazy feet she was holding. The zoo guests learned what an Amur leopard looked like and from the graphics at the zoo that they are indigenous to parts of Russia and northeast China. In nature only 30 of these cats existed in 2007 because of habitat loss and poaching. I learned, and so did zoo guests because they met Nikita and Dimitri, that this is how happy Amur leopards behave. I watched the guests look at each other in astonishment with big smiles on their faces. At that moment, with Nikita and Dimitri's help, they learned, if they had not known before, that leopards feel joy.

The purple flowers on the butterfly bush represent Drek, our female spotted hyena. I would find her resting in purple violets on early summer days. She lived to be 27 years old, one of the longest living hyenas in North America. I can still see her spinning in circles when she saw me coming to visit her. She taught me that you can't judge a book by its cover and that when you are confident you do not need to show your physical strength. She was always patient with me. I recall a wound she had that was the size of pencil eraser under her left eye. I asked the vet if I could train her to allow me to put a topical ointment on it to aid in its healing. He said, "That would be great. Give it a try." I walked to Drek's habitat with betadine cream, a long Q-tip and a bucket of meat. I dipped the 8-inch cotton applicator into the antibiotic ointment, placing a piece of meat in her mouth at the same time I touched her wound with the applicator and talked to her sweetly. Then I put more meat in her complying mouth. Can you believe she did not try to take my Q-tip? She stood there stoic without resistance. I applied the cream twice a day for two weeks and the wound healed. The trust she showed me filled my heart and does to this day. Spotted hyenas have the strongest jaws of all land mammals. She had the ability to inflict damage to the Q-tip, but she chose to be as gentle as possible, allowing me to treat her and allow herself to heal. Female spotted hyenas are one of the most formidable animals in the world and she was generous enough to show me her soft side and gave me her friendship and changed me forever for the better. I bought or borrowed and read every hyena book available the year I met her and her son, Lou, because she made me want to know so much more about her and her kind.

The pink teacup roses in the back left of the garden were planted for sweet Anna and Monty, the mountain lions. They were found and rescued in a park in the state of Montana as young motherless cubs. Female mountain lions do not leave their cubs for extended periods of time. I am sure their mother was unable to return to her precious cubs for some good reason. I have read that humans control mountain lion populations through hunting. Trucks and cars hit these animals on the highways as well. Monty and Anna were hand raised by humans at a zoo and were transferred to our zoo to be representatives of their species and help us educate our zoo guests. Mountain lions have several names; cougar, puma, panther, catamount. We called ours Anna Banana and Monty. Each would come to us quickly no matter what we called them because they were so eager to be with their people. They were both imprinted on humans because of the nurturing they received in their early days and every zookeeper at our zoo adored them and could not wait for the day they were assigned to care for them.

The red roses are for Flounder, always in my heart, teaching me over many years how to be a gentle, effective and fun sea lion trainer. The large bush of daisies in the front of the garden, that blooms in early October, year after year, taller and fuller than the year before, reminds me of the love Puff and I had; but I do not need a reminder, he is unforgettable and forever entwined with my heart. Looking at the flowers, I remember the time I spent loving each animal. The zoo guests and staff appreciate the visual beauty.

When PJ was just two months old, I found him flopping around in the flowers, and like a puppy gone wild, ripping and tearing at the beautiful blooms and foliage. There he was in the garden with a gladiola stalk in his mouth, his little body not much longer than the flower he was attacking, snapping his head back and forth until the stem came free. I was surprised since he was the first sea lion in my care to investigate the garden. He looked at me from fifty yards away with a long flowering stem in his mouth. Now, remember he was only eight weeks old. With a big smile on my face, because he was so-o-o adorable, I said while I shook my fist at him, "Hey! PJ! What are you doing?!" He dove into the pool looking to me like a flamenco dancer with that bright red flower held between his teeth and a glint of mischief in his eye, inviting me to our very first game of keep-away. He thought he had a prize. It amazes me to this day that at two months old he could think that he had something maybe he should not have, consider the situation, and then make the choices he did with that flower. First, he saw the flower from a distance, left the water and entered the garden. He then selected one, grabbed it in his mouth, figured out how to remove it, saw me slide the door open, and when caught in the act, plucked the flower with his teeth while looking at me and quickly decided to take the water route. He kept the flower in his mouth all the while purposely avoiding me and hiding in little caves in his zoo habitat. He knew what he wanted and solved the puzzle of how to obtain it and it was *not* food related. This was for play.

Exercising the sea lions' bodies and minds is an essential part of my job. I am just thrilled when I can think of a new game for them. Initially, new and novel toys would make them leery. It is important for survival in the ocean to avoid something that may not be safe. It did not take them very long to learn that fish might be inside the novel item. I had a blast finding safe and durable containers in which to hide fish. Watching them peek into the hole within the item after they became brave enough to approach it was a highlight in my day. Zoo animal toys need to be heavy-duty and therefore can be very expensive. We never want them to break and possibly harm an animal.

I realized that a plastic watering can will hold up very well in the water (considering they are made for holding water). I purchased all different sizes and colors. My personal favorites were the animal themed watering cans, especially a pink pig. I would cut off the spouts or handles of several of them, making each into a new toy or unique puzzle. I made sure I gave them several at the same time. Every sea lion wanted at least two for themselves. The activity was a great success! The sea lions would swim quickly from watering can to watering can to assess which one would be the easiest for them to get the fish out. The zoo guests and I watched this activity and learned more about sea lion intelligence. At times PJ would take one on land and toss it around with his teeth until a fish popped out. Angel would take one and calmly move it underwater with her flippers until the fish peaked out and she could grab it with her teeth. Star wanted them all to herself, but she quickly learned if she took them all, she would not be getting the fish out as quickly as if she did one at a time. After the watering cans were void of fish the sea lions would swim around quietly by themselves holding the handles or one of them would begin a game of keep-away and have a friend soon hot on their heels darting around the pool. They really enjoyed each other.

I taught Star and PJ to fetch. When the games were done, I would ask them to find the watering cans and bring them to me. To make things more interesting for them, I would bring out a recycling bin and ask the sea lions to deposit them into the bin in exchange for a delicious fish.

Another amusing enrichment idea was a large mirror that I would put in front of the gallery glass so the sea lions could see their reflections. One day, PJ was playing with a few pinecones, when he saw the mirror added to the far side of the gallery glass. I observed him as he gathered the pinecones with his mouth and put some under his flipper and took them to the mirror and watched himself as he released the pinecones and they floated above him. Did you know that sea lions carried items under their flippers? I did not and I have worked with sea lions for many years. PJ once again was learning how his body worked and what he could do like we humans learn. He spent quite a while doing this. I stood at a distance away from the glass and grinned as I took pictures. He knew exactly what he was doing. He realized he could make the reflection change. Did he know the sea lion in the mirror was actually himself? I believe his actions demonstrated it. I have not found much information in my investigation regarding sea lion self-recognition. Self-recognition indicates a higher intelligence; this should be considered an important finding in the science of animal intellect. So much can be learned about how animals think and feel just by observing them: I learned a great deal by giving them the opportunity and taking the time to observe them at play.

One beautiful autumn day, I purchased a large yellow gourd at the public market, about the size of a football. I thought PJ would like the color, the bumpy texture, and the way it would float in the water. I was right. The gourd was extremely buoyant. He spent the entire afternoon trying to keep the gourd underwater with his chin and flippers. PJ was not only enjoying himself immensely, but also getting plenty of exercise moving his new favorite toy all around the pool. Again, I added the mirror to the far side of the gallery glass. PJ pushed his gourd quickly to the mirror to watch the gourd along with his reflection twirling and spinning. Continuously trying to keep that entertaining vegetable under him, he was having a great time learning what he could do with it. Most likely that was the best $2.00 I spent that month. PJ had a blast and I supported a local farmer. What do you think that farmer would say if she knew some of her produce was amusing a sea lion? That would be a good story at the farmer's dinner table!

Whenever I went shopping at a store, I would look at different items and consider if the sea lions would enjoy them somehow. I purchased balls, hula-hoops, and of course, watering cans, to put in their pool as well as objects that lit up that they could observe at the gallery glass. My children were growing up and were not playing with their old toys the way they used to. I brought in their old plastic dinosaurs and stuffed animals for the sea lions to look at through the gallery glass. They seemed to be more interested if the toy moved. I decided to run up and down the length of glass with the toy. Eventually, I would get tired. I experimented using little toy cars to roll back and forth along the 6-inch wide wooden window sill of the gallery glass. This was a BIG hit. I thought if I could just get a second person to receive the car at the other end of the long window sill, the sea lions would be elated. I began to recruit a passing volunteer, zookeeper, docent, or even a zoo visitor to help me with this task. The sea lions had the greatest time following and watching the cars that were crashing into each other, sliding down, or falling off the sill. My human helper would roll it back, the game was on, and we all had a blast. We humans were giggling at our inept car pushing skills and the sea lions were chasing the cars or exhaling and blowing bubbles under water next to the car they wanted us to roll for the next race. Many of the people who took the time to play with the sea lions and me would comment on how they hadn't laughed that hard in a long time. Where else in the world can you interact in play with a wild animal? Here at our zoo our guests have this unique opportunity. I didn't know who was having more fun, the sea lions or the humans. I felt happy that animals and humans were connecting with each other; I firmly believe we are all connected and seeing the joy it brings is one of the many reasons why I love my career.

We zookeepers became more creative with enrichment ideas. We gave the sea lions items to look at that were similar in size but different colors. PJ favored the blue car or paper cutout, asking me with his expelled bubbles when we were at the underwater indoor gallery, to move it again and again. Star preferred yellow colored objects more than any other color of toys offered. She couldn't keep her eyes off any child dressed in yellow. I would find her planted at the gallery glass in front of a child wearing a Sponge-Bob T-shirt. I wondered if this was because the Marine Mammal Care Center's staff and volunteers wore bright yellow rain pants and this color association was a fond memory for her, ironic because in fact they were trying to deter the sea lions from learning that humans were safe. After all, they are shot and injured in other ways by people. I know this because I volunteered at the same rescue center and that is the protocol. Angel seemed to be drawn more frequently to the red toy, continually staring at the red car or ball when I lined up various cars, balls or paper hearts on the sill of the gallery glass for her to choose which one I would move next for her. Articles I have read about sea lions and their vision do not suggest sea lions see colors as well as Star, Angel and PJ were proving to me and our guests, that their color vision may be more complex than once considered. Their vision must be studied further in a comfortable, playful atmosphere similar to where our sea lions live because a stress free environment would yield the best data on color perception in sea lions. I was learning more and more each day about these animals as individuals.

Back in the 1990s, my mother collected battery-operated singing fish. They became one of the most entertaining items for the sea lions and me. She did not have a use for them now, but I thought I knew who might enjoy them. I recall the first day I set one of these animatronic fish on the sill of the gallery glass for the sea lions to look at. The great thing about this toy is that it has a motion sensor. These fish replicas move and sing when someone or something moves in front of it. I could not believe how quickly all three sea lions learned that they could turn it on. When I set it up for the first time the sea lions came over to look at this newest item of interest. The fish began opening its mouth and a tune began. I knew they could hear the song because I could hear through the gallery glass the sound of their expelled bubbles as they exhaled in gleeful surprise. All three floated underwater trying to understand what they were looking at while the fish continued belting out its song. When the fish stopped moving and singing, three very still sea lions, lined up in a row underwater, in front of this toy. One of them moved enough for the fish to begin its next song and its tail began wiggling. I laughed at their surprise as I watched them expel more bubbles and then look at each other under water and in wonder at the fish. It looked to me as if they were asking each other about this weird fish because I saw questions in their eyes. I couldn't help but smile and with a warm feeling in my heart, I went on to my other duties.

I came back a few hours later to see if they were still interested in the fish. It would have been the most successful toy we had ever given them, if they still were playing with it. When I entered the Rocky Coasts inside galley, I saw a docent observing the sea lions. We made small talk and I told him about the fish. He told me he watched Angel swim over to the fish every time it stopped singing until the toy began dancing and belting out its tune once again. But the battery wore out! I was thrilled! I asked my mom if she had an adapter to plug into the electric outlet so they could have fun with it as long as they wanted. She did! It is those small things in life that I have learned to appreciate.

I tried to think of new and creative ways to use each enrichment item. Would the sea lions enjoy watching themselves play with the fish in a mirror? With the sea lions watching that silly fish wiggle and sing, I added the mirror once again directly behind the fish and in front of them. I saw their attention brighten as they looked at their own reflections along with the reflections of their peers and that goofy fish. Then as they each looked at the toy, then themselves, and then at each other in the mirror, or as they turned to look at one another, I was in stitches with laughter. Absolutely, this was another success. One day I brought the fish out, plugged in the cords, and set up the mirror. PJ swam over quickly to the fish and then left to tell Star it was there. I saw him find Star and signal to her to follow him. She was sleeping at the time and reluctantly opened her eye. She looked over to where the fish sat silently on the window sill and fell back to sleep. PJ then glanced at the toy and swam off, obviously only wanting to play with the singing fish if it were with a sea lion friend, but Star said, "No."

Watching them have fun and observing them learn as they were trying to understand something new, changed my life and who I became professionally. I comprehended that because they had bountiful amounts of fish, each other, were healthy, and felt safe, they had the luxury to play and learn. If they had been concerned about their safety because they did not get along, or they were hungry, or ill, they would not play. We only play when our basic needs are met and when we are comfortable with our surroundings.

Chapter 3
Making Each Day Better

Lou, the happy hyena

I am often asked about my duties as a zookeeper. Enrichment and training are very important aspects of my job, but there is much more that happens within a single day. I just got home from work and although no two days are alike, I will outline what occurred today. Yesterday we had a snowstorm; we received 16 inches of blowing snow. The zoo remained opened so all the walkways needed to be shoveled and salted for our staff to get around and our zoo's guests to trek about and observe our animals as they enjoy a fresh snowfall. We zookeepers shovel a lot. But that was yesterday. On this January morning we had freezing rain which covered the city's roads, our cars and the animals' habitats. I arrived at the zoo before the sun rose. I pulled into the zoo's parking lot. In the darkness with the snow and ice covered asphalt I mis-parked, creating a new spot all my own. Exiting my car I stepped on the lake of ice that encased the parking lot. My foot slipped and I giggled thinking it was going to take me a very long time to walk the half mile to the Rocky Coasts' diet kitchen. Last year I fell on my rump in a similar situation, denting the soup can that was in the bag that landed under me. As I looked for an iceless area to help determine my route to the time clock, a coworker exited his car; the wind picked up and blew him a few feet across the lot. I watched him slip-slide passed my car as we laughed. It took me about a million baby steps to walk that slick half mile before my workday could begin.

We had our daily morning team meeting and discussed animal health issues as well as future demonstrations to educate our guests. I was assigned the care of Katya, our 13-year old Amur tiger, Lou, our 26-year old spotted hyena, and our four-year old Grey wolf siblings, Willow and Timber, as well as helping with the feeding and training of our California sea lions. I was also asked to assist in the training of our female polar bear for injections because she was scheduled to be artificially inseminated in a few weeks. This would be the third time this polar bear was inseminated. We are hoping this time science has improved and a cub would be born in November. Polar bears are critically endangered in nature. They are starving and drowning in the Arctic because the ice caps on which they must stand to hunt seals are disappearing due to global warming. Our zoo is helping every way it can to keep these beautiful top predators on earth as long as possible. In 2012, our zoo's polar bear was the first polar bear in the world to be artificially inseminated! Aurora allowed me to hand inject her multiple times with hormone primer to prepare her to become pregnant and then allowed me to inject her with medication that anesthetized her. Our male polar bear, Zero, (named because he was born on a subzero day) also allowed me to hand inject him with the help of our zoo's veterinarian. We used two syringes and administered them at the same time because the amount of medication was over 6 ml and we were not sure Zero would sit still for as long as it takes to receive it. We used Zero's sperm which our vet staff helped him donate. Our zoo made the history books and helped science understand this process and polar bears even more, even though it did not result in a cub. Now, seven years later, Aurora's first cub, Anoki, is back at this zoo following in her mother's footsteps and hopefully will be the first polar bear impregnated through artificial insemination.

The first thing we do every day as zookeepers is check the health of each animal in our care; then we inventory their habitat for any enclosure compromises such as tree issues or electric or plumbing malfunctions. Katya and Lou are "senior citizens" at the zoo. Amur tigers and spotted hyenas, on average, each live to be 12 years old. Katya acts feisty while playing and enjoys learning new behaviors. You would never guess by looking at her she was at the end of her life span. Lou on the other hand is 26 years old—the oldest spotted hyena in North America, quite possibly the world. He knows 23 behaviors learned through positive reinforcement training. I have never corrected him for an error in learning. I realize that if he does not understand what I am teaching him it is because I am not conveying to him correctly what I am asking him to do. It is never the animal's fault if there is a miscommunication between teacher and student. It is the teacher's obligation to learn how to communicate with the animal.

Lou and Katya are both on glucosamine for their aging joints. We hide these pills in their daily meat or sometimes fish. If they happen to pick them out, we hide them again until they receive the dose our zoo veterinarian recommends. While they are eating, I check the inside of their mouth, their coat, each body part, and assess their overall well-being by their interest, mobility, and appetite. Once I determine the tiger, wolves, and hyena are healthy and safe, I return to the diet kitchen and meet up with the sea lion team. We call the sea lions into their inside holding, lock them inside for a moment and check their overall health and well-being. We trained the sea lions to come inside three times a day in case there is a pool malfunction, a weather issue, such as subzero weather or a blizzard, a filter issue, or a glass compromise. Our zoo animals need to come to us when called to be safe. Their lives depend on it.

Our sea lions get a multivitamin daily hidden in their fish. Sea lions eat fish whole because they do not have molars; their teeth are for ripping and tearing. In their natural range all their nutrition and water comes from the fish that they eat. Sea lions naturally do not drink ocean water because the ocean is salt water, of course.

We taught our sea lions to open their mouths and hold them open so we can check gum color and teeth integrity. They also get a vitamin E supplement along with a pinniped eye vitamin supplement. All of these are hidden within their fish. After our diet prep and training, we document for each sea lion the amount of food they ate, their response during the session, the vitamins they received, and their eye quality.

We clean the fish buckets (each sea lion has his or her own designated bucket) and we transfer boxes of fish from the freezer to the refrigerator for the next day. Thawing takes approximately 24 hours. The sea lions receive a variety of fish. The fish comes frozen in boxes which we store in a walk-in freezer. We thaw it out daily so the animals receive the best quality possible. Capelin and herring are given every day. Mackerel and squid are offered at different times of the year depending on the season and how much fat they need; we switch from mackerel in winter to squid in the summer.

We also thaw different varieties of meat for some of the other animals for the following day. Whole chickens, chicken backs, chicken gizzards, turkey necks, ground horse which is created for zoo carnivores and is fortified with vitamins, horse chunks, goat heads, cow legs, cow heads, pork legs, and venison from the deer that live in our area. The police will drop off a fresh killed deer from the highway. Our vet inspects the donation for potential bullets or health issues the deer may have had prior to their accidental deaths before we feed our carnivores the freshest of meat.

After 30 plus years of working at the zoo, I can't begin to guess how many dead animals I have seen, yet alone touched, while preparing the animals' diets. I see the meat and fish now as my friends the sea lions, wolves, tiger, and hyena see it. The sea lions receive between 10 to 20 pounds of fish a day each. Katya is given up to 15 pounds of many meat varieties. Lou's diet consists of three pounds of meat and he also enjoys corn on the cob and the occasional cucumber. Our wolves get three cups of wolf chow, which is a fortified dry food (it looks like dog kibble) and two and a half pounds of meat each. I look forward to surprising them with the variety and the presentation just like when I prepare a meal at home, minus the cooking part. That is where environmental enrichment comes in to play. It is one of our goals as zookeepers– to have the animals in our care explore and use their natural skills to obtain their food for the day, every day.

After the sea lions' first feeding of the day, I prepare the grey wolves' morning diet and head over to their habitat where I see them see me and they dash off to hide; then I hide and we bound playfully towards each other in a game of "who saw who first?" They play bow, give a little whine, and I run off like a wounded animal, laughing, to meet them in the back of their habitat for their injection training. I reinforce their behavior with meat when their shoulders come near the fence where I am standing. They are inside their habitat and I am directly on the other side of the fencing. It is possible to train animals without being in their habitats. Katya Tiger has learned ten behaviors, including allowing us to inject her with vaccines that our zoo vet wants her to have to keep her healthy. She allowed us for the first time to tranquilize her for a full examination this year. This means she could not be reinforced with food after her injection. Lou Hyena knows twenty-three behaviors. He also was tranquilized this year for a tooth extraction. Positive reinforcement training, when done correctly, builds enormous trust with the animals for their people. Image the trust it would take a wild animal to have to allow a human to put a needle into their muscle. They choose to participate. This is amazing to witness let alone participate in.

I have never entered Katya or Lou's areas when they were in them. It is possible to communicate what the desired behavior is without contact. Just following me when I call them is the first step. Becoming their playmate really helped strengthen the trust-building aspect. Positive reinforcement training has not let us down yet. I am hopeful someday the wolves will allow me to inject them too when they need their annual vaccines. Time will tell. Until then we will have a lot of fun and build a trusting relationship. I have read and witnessed that there are as many ways to train an animal as there are people training animals. The safe, fun and humane way is absolutely the way to go.

After the wolves' training, I lock them out of the area where their beds and water are so I can safely enter. I give them fresh water and clean their beds. Today I will hide horse femur bones in paper bags within their dens. These bones come in frozen and they weigh about 10 pounds each and are as long as my leg. Afterwards, I lock up the gates so the wolves again have access to their entire habitat. They find the bags, rip them open, and bound away with the bones, carrying them with ease. I once read that female wolves can eat up to twenty pounds of meat in a sitting so they can carry it to their pups and regurgitate it for them. Talk about a mother's love. Willow and Timber are sister and brother; to prevent them breeding Timber was neutered. They came from a litter of nine, so their genes are well represented in the zoo population.

Next, I oil all the locks and pulleys on the gates. Maintaining their function in the winter is imperative. Frozen locks and gates that will not open make really cold winter days very long.

Lou Hyena is in the space next to the wolves' habitat. When our zoo's Mexican wolves were relocated to a breeding program to help reestablish their population in their natural range, the longtime wolf yard was vacant for a while. This area and Lou's habitat was separated by a fence. For enrichment, we decided to give Lou access to the area to investigate. I called to him as I waited one hundred yards away. He had to go through gates he had never passed through before into an area he was unfamiliar with. I stood there alone calling, "Come on big buddy!" Lou was cautious, as he should be, entering a potentially dangerous situation. The unknown always has potential hazards for all of us. It didn't take long before I saw him coming from his yard around the bend into the new yard. He momentarily sniffed his surroundings and then headed straight to his crazy friend cheering him on. He would come to me anytime I asked. I can see his eyes sparkling as I write this. We would find him basking in the sun throughout the day as he enjoyed his new digs.

Soon after, our zoo acquired Timber and Willow and Lou returned to his original habitat. There was a stockade fence along with a chain link fence separating the two species. The wolves were extremely timid and tried to keep to themselves. I would find Lou peeking through the cracks of the wooden fence to get a look at his new neighbors and from time to time I would find a six-foot length of the fence rearranged by Lou. He would pull off one of the slats and I would hammer the piece of wood back in place giggling to myself. Then Lou began to take entire planks of wood and drag them one hundred feet inside to his den. I observed the wolves trot away from their nosy neighbor a couple of times. We decided then to get a hole saw and make some peek holes for Lou. Now that his curiosity was satiated, we would see him watching the wolves being trained even though I made sure Lou always had his training session first. I make sure I visit each animal in my care several times a day for training and enrichment. This brightens their days and mine.

After Lou heard me with the wolves, he was ready for his turn for food and fun once again. He met me at the fencing spinning in circles. His mouth would be open and he would be panting joyfully, his tail swishing back and forth. He has done this when excited since the day I met him in 2006. I put "spin" on a cue so he does this when I ask him also. Spin is one of the twenty-three behaviors Lou knows. First, he was taught his name. He learned this was by giving him meat when his name was said. Soon his name meant a delicious meatball. I would go to different places on the outside of his habitat and say his name and immediately give him food when he came to me. He is fed every time he does what he is asked. He learned recall and to be locked in and out of his den area this way. Lou would follow me anywhere. We always had fun together. If he looks forward to being with me half as much as I like our time together, I would be thrilled.

Next Lou learned to go on a weight board. Initially he picked up the plywood piece and walked off with it. Soon he realized placing his feet on it was the action I desired. I use a clicker to capture a precise moment in time. The click sound is paired with food over and over again. Soon an animal knows food is on its way and the action they just did is the one I am asking them for. Lou puts his side against the fence when he is excited in play. This

41

behavior I captured with the clicker and put it on a cue. We call this "side up." We could use this posture for an injection if needed. We haven't yet because he does this in play and I do not want to "ruin" our fun when an injection is needed. I put together a little chute made with his water tub flipped upside down with a space for his body next to the fence mesh. Lou was taught to enter this area and hold still while being touched. Soon he was allowing us to inject him.

He was taught to target a target pole, a stick with a softball-sized ball at the end. We can shape behaviors with this tool. He was given a click and food when he touched his nose to the object on the opposite side of the fence around his habitat.

Lou has a 50-gallon, 16-inch high, 4-foot long stock tank (when his old tub sprung a leak a new one was donated by Maureen, one of his ZooParents. I ordered it on Amazon and had it sent to the zoo addressed to Lou Hyena; he's probably the only animal at the zoo to ever have a package delivered to him. I'm sure it must have made many people smile when it was announced over the two-way radio, "Package for Lou Hyena.") He enjoys soaking in his tub on hot days. I thought it would be a great idea at the summer demonstration, where people learn about hyenas for a half an hour on Wednesday afternoons, that zoo guests also be able to learn about positive reinforcement training.

People occasionally force their dogs to take baths. In the past I have picked up my 60-pound dog and carried her to the tub for a bath. She was afraid to go in by herself. It was a task I wanted over as soon as possible, so I just got through the process. I would tell her she was good, but neither of us enjoyed ourselves during her bath. This is a common practice, but not necessary.

Through approximations I taught Lou to go into his tub. At first, I put small pieces of fish or chicken in his tub. When that caught his attention and he looked into the tub, I clicked and gave him food. When one paw went in, I cheered and clicked and gave him food. When he looked in my eyes, put another paw directly in the tub, I said "YAY! GOOD, BOY!" (By the way, he most likely thinks his name is "Good boy-Lou") clicked once more and gave him more meat. Now that he was half in, I directed his nose with a fish and his third foot went in. "Almost there," I thought. I said, "Let's go, Buddy." On dry land that means to move with me forward. He moved up the couple inches that brought that last foot in; now he was standing in the tub. I cheered and fed him more. He is allowed up to three pounds of meat a day. We vary how he receives it, offering it by hiding it throughout the yard just once a day, or throughout the day, or during training.

The next day I wondered if he would remember what we did the day before. It was another hot summer day. I would not ask him to go into water if it was cold. His health is the number one priority. He and I met at his tub each on different sides of the fence. I plunked a chicken gizzard in the water. He looked at the water then me, then a paw in! I said, "Good boy, that is right! Go in, Buddy." He walked right into the cool water and I gave him a raw chicken drumstick. We practiced this fun "game" on hot days and I began to gently hose his back while he opened his mouth in delight, flicking the water with his tail which cooled me off at the same time. Children came and watched the happy hyena playing in the water. He was so close to the fence that when he began flopping around side to side, he made waves and with his tail splashed water four feet into the visitors' walkway. The children screeched and laughed and I commented, "Where else in the world can you get cooled off by a splashing hyena?" ("And safely," I thought secretly to myself.) Lou stayed in that tub next to me for twenty minutes apparently having a very good time amazing our zoo guests. They didn't know how much fun a hyena could have and that they feel joy. Lou jumped out of the tub, shook the water off, and darted around his yard much like my dogs do after they get a bath. Then he acted like nothing happened and plopped

43

down in his straw bed in the sun to dry off. A zoo guest arrived at Lou's area and commented, "All that hyena ever does is relax in the sun." The children and I, who were soaked, looked at each other and laughed. It wasn't long before Lou would enter the tub when I said, "tub." It was wonderful to show people this at Lou's demo.

Lou was never forced to do anything, including going into his tub. He is convinced by kindness and treats. Guests would laugh and say, "What am I supposed to do, give my dog raw chicken in the bath tub?" I said, "If you want to, but hot dog slices work at my house for my dogs." I remind people that Lou is not a dog; he is a hyena, a wild animal. If he can learn with patience and treats so can your domesticated dog at home. Kindness goes a long way.

I taught Lou to fetch and now, because of training, he knows the difference between his ball, a stick, or a novel item. A novel item is anything other than his ball or stick. Like at the sea lions, items blow into their habitats or get thrown in by people who do not value the animals' lives as much as they should. Lou is quite possibly the only hyena in the world that retrieves items.

I taught Lou, the wolves, and the tigers how to respond to an emergency recall. This is necessary in case of an emergency and we need them to leave their den areas immediately. They also know a recall to go into their den areas as fast as they can in the event we need them to leave their habitat to secure them in their holding areas. I pair the whistle sound with a delicious treat; I use fatty pork. Now the whistle means fatty pork and they can't wait for that!

Lou knows his emergency recall—two loud toots on a whistle. Hearing the sound, he runs as fast as he can to a destination I specified during his training, a spot at the front of his yard. When he first learned this recall, I practiced with him to see how strong the behavior was. I would sneak over to his area. If he knew I was there it would not be a surprise like an emergency would be. One time I hid behind a bush in the front of his habitat. I did not know where he was and he was about to get some fatty pork if he came to the correct area quickly. I blew the whistle and looked towards his den expecting he was resting there. I saw a rustling in the back right bush and here comes Lou like a freight train, squatting in the middle of making a poop! Poor guy! He got a lot of pork for that. I conducted another test in a rain storm. He heard the toot and dashed from his den in the pouring rain to his crazy, very wet friend who had a pound of pork waiting for him. In the morning, evening, snow, and rain, Lou responded very quickly to the whistle. Now we knew he would be safe if he needed to be locked in his den because of enclosure compromise or his den area needed to be vacated for any reason.

One day my supervisor was walking by and asked how Lou was doing (by the way, everyone loves Lou because of his zest for life). It was a warm summer's day and he was snoozing on his beloved straw bed. I said, "Do you want to see his emergency recall?" She said, "Okay." I blew the whistle and he popped up from a dead sleep with straw strands in his hair, almost falling over to get to his spot! He was probably still dreaming as he ate his pork. He was really cute with his bed head. Cute=hyena. Not something most people would equate, but it is the truth.

Now that we are the subject of hyena and dreams, I will share this. I was weeding in front of his habitat, (yes, zookeepers at my zoo do a lot of ground maintenance) and Lou was sound asleep on his yard's straw bed. I stopped my task for a quick back stretch and began to talk to our zoo guests about hyenas in general when Lou, eye's closed, flat on his side, began moving his legs slightly and his lips and cheeks began filling with air slightly. One zoo guest commented that her dog dreams that way too. She was right, Lou was dreaming, twitching and puffing he was running somewhere. We watched him and felt wonder. Why would we be surprised that Lou dreams? It is strange that when you actually witness

45

something it is much easier to believe. We watched silently for about twenty minutes, longer than any zoo guest will typically stay in front of one of our animals' habitats on average. I said to our guests, "Now you will have a fun discussion around the family dinner table tonight."

Hyenas have at least fourteen documented vocalizations. They have a complex society and each noise they make sounds unique from each individual and means something completely different to each member of the clan. Many days at approximately 4 p. m., Lou would begin "whooping." This was a low and deep call and he faced the ground or a wall in his den while doing it, I am guessing, to make it carry further. If we were lucky, Katya would begin roaring her territorial call, telling all tigers in our area this was her home. If we were very fortunate, the Canada lynx would answer and they would form a choir; we would all stop and listen to this with awe.

On another occasion a zoo educator was walking with me as we passed by Lou's habitat. Lou began vocalizing, "Whoop-Whoop." I said to the educator, "It is Lou's clan call; let's go to him" We were smiling because it was an adventure and we couldn't wait to see how he responded to our arrival. I unlocked a stockade fence that leads to Lou's dens and holding areas. I said, "Here we come, buddy!" We didn't hear a response so we peeked through his den's back window. Lou was sound asleep! Did you know spotted hyena vocalized in their sleep? Well, they do. And I, after working with him for 13 years, did not know it until that day. I am learning more and more to pay attention to the world around me and not get too caught up in the mundane things in life.

When Lou was younger, he would grow impatient when the keepers were servicing his den. I knew this because after he ate his food reward for switching into the other area, he would begin tossing his head in frustration. I taught him an incompatible behavior. This is an activity he could learn and do while he was

46

waiting where he couldn't toss his head. I taught him to go around a tree while he waited for me to clean his den. Now when he is impatient, he makes a loop around the tree. I toss him a bunch of goodies and usually that satisfies him. He seems to enjoy this behavior and he learned it quickly so I thought "why don't we try it on the other side while I am cleaning the other den?" Sure enough, when I asked him to "go around," he looked at me and made a loop around a log in his small holding area. "Smart Louie," I said. We went a step further. There is a 16-foot log out in his yard. It took a few training sessions, but now Lou goes around that log. He then learned to go around a large rock.

When he was younger, he would stand up on his hind legs when we asked. It's too dangerous now because his body is slowing down and noticeably weaker. He allows us to touch him with a backscratcher; this will help if we ever need to treat a wound topically. He also paints. His beautiful paw prints are sold at our Animal Art Expo once a year to help raise money for conservation efforts. Last, but not least, Lou lets us spray him with an organic liquid commonly used for horses that repels mosquitos, flies, fleas and ticks. Most animals including humans do not like to be squirted with a spray bottle. Lou doesn't mind anymore and the insects leave him alone on summer days and nights.

Completing my work at Lou's den, I give him fresh water and add a 50-pound bag of pine shavings after removing the soiled bedding. I check the weather on my phone. A low of 9 degrees is predicted for tonight so I add a bale of straw too. Lou has four heaters, three bales of straw, and three bags of shavings. This combination should keep his den 50 degrees throughout the freezing night. His den is cozy and when I am home, I will think of him curled up all toasty under the heaters and a thick soft bed of straw. He deserves the best we can give him.

In early October 2018, Lou appeared to have an issue with his mouth. On October 19, 2018, he allowed me to hand inject him with medicine to anesthetize him. He came over when I called him like thousands of times before and allowed me to touch him, this time with a needle. Our zoo veterinarian gave him a full physical, found an abscessed tooth, pulled it and Lou was back in the game soon after. Years ago, an abscessed tooth would have cost Lou his life. With excellent health care and compassionate training Lou may have many years ahead of him.

On May 11, 2019, Lou was the first hyena to have a cataract removed. He came to me like he always has and allowed me to hand inject him once again. The trust he has for me can only be compared to the love I have for him. While he was recovering after the surgery and still asleep, I was rubbing his back and found a small growth, the size of a pencil eraser. I showed the zoo vet and he showed me two teeth that needed to be removed next time Lou was anesthetized. The eye surgery did not improve his eyesight as well as we had hoped. On June 8, 2019, the eye surgeons wanted to treat Lou's eye with injections to his eyelid; these injections would promote healing of the eye. Lou came to me with very little vision, and I hand injected him once again. While we had Lou under anesthesia, his two broken teeth were removed and the growth on his back which had grown five times the size of a pencil's eraser within three weeks was also removed and a sample was sent out for a biopsy.

At the time I am writing this story, Lou's vision is not as good as it was prior to the cataract surgery. Part of me wants to get frustrated that Lou had to undergo so much for something that may not help him in the end. Again, there are no coincidences and everything happens for a reason. When the report came back on the biopsy, the growth was identified as cancer. I am not a doctor, but consider this, if that tumor multiplied five times more in three more weeks, it would have been in his spine in no time. So unintendedly the cataract surgery saved his life.

Every Day Is a Gift

On June 18 2019, Lou allowed me to give him eye drops for the first time. For ten days I put steroid/antibiotic medicine in his eye three drops at a time, one to three times a day. He never refused, always willing for some delicious meat treat. Yes, his vision began to improve. He allowed me to help him, thereby helping himself. But, in mid-July, Lou's eye began to look cloudy. The eye surgeon recommended Lou received sixteen eye drops a day for two weeks. Lou allowed me to do this every day every time I asked until July 31. He would not come to me and looked uncomfortable for the first time. I told the zoo vet that Lou would not come to me so I could not help him that day. The decision was made to remove Lou's eye.

The day after the surgery I came in early because I needed to see how Lou was faring. He saw me and went to his gate in his yard. He was telling me he wanted to go out to his yard. He could see me! He felt well enough to communicate to me his needs. My supervisor was there and the vet was on his way to check Lou's postoperative health. I was told I could give Lou access to his yards. He went in and out of the doors of his habitat with ease, going around and around as if he wanted to prove his vision to us. I didn't think I could be any prouder of him and his "I'm-a-survivor" attitude. He went to his straw bed in his yard and fluffed it up with his paws and with his zookeeper friends watching and hugging each other, he came right back to where I was kneeling. At that moment it was declared this was our best morning meeting to date.

I watched my coworkers smile and pat each other on their backs saying to each other they never expected anything as wonderful as a bright and eager Lou the day after such a surgery. I turned away from my departing coworkers and looked into Lou's shiny brown eye and said, "Good boy, Lou; I love you, buddy." I examined the area where his right eye had been and stayed with him until he wandered out to his yard again to explore.

Animal/human relationships are beautiful when built with trust and love.

Getting back to that cold day in January, next, I visit Katya the Amur tiger. She is lying low, stalking me. I enter her storage barn carrying paper bags and cardboard boxes, dropping and tossing them all over as I hide inside the building, getting her excited by my actions, and indicating she is about to have a bit of fun and get some food. The boxes and bags are for enrichment; she enjoys destroying these after I fill them with meat. I am purposely throwing and dropping them as I make my entrance for the purpose of entertaining her. She prances into her inside holding area animated and ready for fun. I know she is a top predator and voted one of the most dangerous animals at our zoo by our staff, but we can still have the kind of fun she likes because we never come in contact with each other.

We sometimes hang deer carcasses for her to feed on, along with scented boxes for her to tear. She enjoys pumpkin pie spice and will roll all over in it with zest. I have seen her chase and catch chipmunks and squirrels. Most recently she caught a screech owl; poor little owl chose the wrong area of the zoo to rest. Katya was born at our zoo along with her brother Ussuri and sister Anastasia. She is not recommended to breed from the Species Survival Plan because her mother had many cubs and their bloodline therefore is well represented in the gene pool.

After I clean Katya's yard and add scents and food for her to discover, I head back to the sea lion area for their second feeding. On my way back I stop at the underwater viewing area to play with them and observe their behavior. Who is interacting with whom? Have they found a stick or pinecone to start a game with? I take a seat and watch a sea lion game of tag. He is it; no, she is it. They are getting great amounts of exercise learning from one another in play. I leave them to their fun and get their diets ready for this feeding; we call them inside as usual and give them overall health assessments, then have a little fun. We clean up and get ready to head out to our lunch. Before leaving, I work at the computer documenting the sea lions' sessions as well as the enrichment and training with Katya, Lou, and the wolves that I have done thus far today.

After I document the morning's activities, I play with the sea lions at the gallery glass. Today I use a small toy car and a tennis ball. They chase it up and down the window sill and blow bubbles underwater to ask me to do it again. I know every time I have a positive experience with the sea lions our relationship grows, but I am doing this because it is fun for us too.

Lunch is over and the next thing on my to-do list is to weigh Katya. It took me a few months to train her to go on the weight board. We teach our animals to be weighed so that we can calculate the precise dose of medicine for their exact weight. She is a high fear animal, meaning she is leery of anything different; this includes the wooden board which I put in her habitat for her to stand on. In the past she ran around flipping over any novel item. She needed to learn not to do this at weighing time. I did this by first training her to step on cardboard calmly. Cardboard is cheap and would not harm her if she decided she did not want to be calm. With boneless chicken and pork, I reinforced her gentle ways and calm acceptance when the cardboard was present. A few days later I covered the weight board with cardboard then clicked and fed her when her large paws slowly and deliberately went where I asked, on the board. After I was pretty sure she was desensitized to this routine, I added the scale.

Each time after I called her into her holding area and she was secured safely inside, I entered her outdoor habitat where I would set up the board and cardboard. It was strange because she watched me set everything up—the frightening board and scary scale. Then I would cover it with cardboard. I would secure her habitat after I exited, then open the gate that lets her into her yard.

I would click and reinforce as she trotted over to the scale. One paw, one chicken breast, two paws another piece of meat, until she was calmly looking at me and gently taking meat from my tongs. She took my breath away looking at me, trusting me to do something that a month ago was just an idea that I turned into a training plan. She weighed 262 pounds. This is small for an Amur tiger. They are the largest of the big cats. She is petite and at a healthy weight.

Now I need to get Katya off her beloved board and follow me back inside so I can take the scale and board out of her yard. If left in the yard with her, she would most likely destroy it and possibly harm herself if she decided to chew it. This is where her recall comes in handy. I teach the animals this first before I go any farther in their training. It is imperative they come when I need them to. Since I reinforced Katya for standing on that board a LOT, she looked at me oddly when I asked her to follow me inside. I called her and said "let's go!" Then went to the door I wanted her to enter. One moment, two moments and she left the board with a leap and pranced inside. I shut the door and took a breath and I gave her a big chunk of meat.

She doesn't have to do as I say. With positive reinforcement training, the animal is requested to do something. If they oblige, great things are on the way. If I ever thought to punish someone as sensitive as Katya, I could never get the trust I have with her now. Not the trust to enter her habitat. Oh, no; I am not fool enough to risk my life. I know where I belong and it is not in a top predator's home. When I enter her habitat, I always have a little twinge of anxiety because I understand she was just in there and one mistake means my life. I remove the scales and hide a few bags with meat inside in the trees of her habitat. I let her out into the yard and she goes around looking to see what I just did. I leave her to her enrichment and go back to the computer to document her weight and enrichment and get ready for the final sea lion feeding.

Every Day Is a Gift

Last year our zoo veterinarian wanted a full physical on Katya. Katya's twin sister, Anastasia, passed away from cancer over a year ago so of course Katya is at a greater risk because they shared the same genetics and environment. On September 18, 2018, Katya came over to me like she did every day and I hand injected her. She was asleep in minutes. After her physical, the blood work came back and there was a problem with her liver. She was put on a daily oral medicine and still trusts me to this day, albeit it took her a couple days to forgive me for the needle stick. Raw pork convinced her I was indeed her friend.

Like clockwork, the sea lions come when they are called. Everyone gets a quick eye check and body appraisal and new toys to play with at the end of the day. I document all of this and head to the wolves and Lou for their last meal of the day. I call the wolves to me and reinforce this recall, then toss bits of meat throughout their yard for them to find later. I check their locks and gates and refill water bowls. Louie is waiting for me too. It is cold out so I don't ask him to go out into his yard. This geriatric African animal is better near his warm den. I check his locks and gates and give him a pound of meat which he takes inside his den to savor. I toss three pounds of meat over Katya's fence into her yard for her to find at her leisure (it is the last of the fifteen pounds she received this day), and check her locks and gates and refill her water. I meet up with my team because this is the end of the day and we check each other's safety. We walk up the icy road together knowing tomorrow will go just as fast as this day did. No two days are ever the same; this has been true the last thirty years and I don't expect it to change. Every single day we try to make the next day better for the animals than the day before because they deserve it. And, of course, we never know when it might be our last day with them.

On October 19, 2019, I received a call from work telling me Lou was not well and to see if I could come as soon as possible. At

Every Day Is a Gift

27 years and 16 days old I knew the end was near for my friend. Not many people have been fortunate to have a friend like Lou for so many years and I never took that for granted. I looked in my cupboard and found a can of chicken; I put that in my pocket along with a can opener. Always bring the right tools for the job. The can needed to be opened and Lou needed me.

When I arrived at work I was met by our zoo's vet and we walked to Lou's habitat to evaluate his health. I looked at him quickly and could tell he was uncomfortable by the way he was laying. I didn't want him to see me yet, because if he came to me now, perhaps for the last time, he may not have been able to get up again. First, I wanted to have everything to help him ready for immediate use.

Our staff filled me in and said he was weak and falling over. These are zoo professionals and if they said Lou looked like he was suffering, I believed them 100%. I wanted Lou to go to heaven without stress or fear. If I could give him the medicine to sedate him while he was eating his favorite canned chicken, it would be our final gift of love for each other. He heard me talking and stood up weakly to greet me. I said, "Hey, buddy, have you been falling down? You are the best boy in the world." He pushed the tip of his nose out of the fencing and I gave it a kiss. Lou's zookeeper friends each came over and each told him they loved him. Then the vet arrived with the medicine syringe and I asked if I could be the one to give Lou the injection just as we'd trained for.

However, Lou's injection area had to be set up. There is a pyramid-shaped object that we place near the fencing that brings his shoulder closer to me. He needed to go to his switch area so we could put it in place. I put some treats in his switch area and with great effort he made it to the treats; the door was shut and I moved the wedge into position. While I was placing it, Lou fell over on his side twice. I was not sure if he would be able to get up to come to me or ever get up again. We opened the gate between switch yards

54

and I began calling him back to me. He stood up and walked this way and that, unbalanced, but determined, trying to find me in the place I have fed him thousands of times.

I absolutely knew it was his time. I began giving him little chunks of the canned chicken with my left hand. He was licking the morsels as I was praising his efforts and telling him how much I loved him just like I did every time I saw him. I picked up the syringe with my right hand and slowly and gently gave him the medicine. He never flinched as I continued feeding and loving him. He stepped away unsteadily and laid down right next to me. I picked up the backscratcher and softly rubbed him, murmuring "rub-a-dub-rub-a-dub," tears pouring down my face. After he was asleep, we entered his holding area. I knelt down and hugged him and butterflied kissed him. I knew he knew I was there because his lips twitched. I did not cry while hugging and kissing him. Even on medication I did not want him to wonder why I was sad.

We carried him to a golf cart and took him to our animal hospital. His people stood around him as I hugged and kissed him. There he was humanely euthanized. We hugged each other and cried at our loss. I felt him pass under my hands as he went to his new home and into the hands of our Lord. I felt the Lord's love and I visualized him saying, "Good job, Lou; great job bringing all these people together because they loved you."

People called and texted me from all over the world. Some were my family and some were Lou's friends or my friends. Lou was greatly loved by many. My advice to anyone who wants it (ha ha ha): Take time to love the hyenas in your life. You won't be sorry you did.

Chapter 4
Fish is Food, PJ

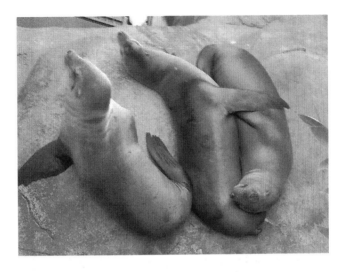

Angel with spooning Star and PJ

Weaning PJ was a painstaking process to say the least. It took two months for PJ to start eating fish because he had no interest in it. He still wanted mom's milk, but Star did not have enough milk for this big pup. By this time in nature he would have had to start looking for fish on his own. If they lived in the wild, Star would have left PJ for days at a time in a cave or on a beach while she hunted for fish. Then like other pups he would have become very hungry and tried to find something to eat. This does not happen at zoos. Star did not have to swim for days in search of fish to eat. Research has shown that mothers do not teach their pups how to hunt. The pup's natural hunting instinct kicks in when they grow hungry enough and they learn to hunt by themselves. Well, Star never read that chapter in the sea lion manual either. On a few occasions, during her routine feedings she would call PJ to us and give him a fish with her mouth and he would swim away and play with it. Star amazed me, always doing her own thing and what she decided was important at the time. Incredible! Star had watched me offer fish to PJ countless times and he would not eat it. Why would she give her food away? Given the opportunity she would attempt to take a fish from any other sea lion. Sea lions are opportunistic eaters. She may have thought there was a better chance he would eat from her, or perhaps she was trying to please me. Your guess is as good as mine, but I was astounded nonetheless. Behavior like this that I have observed is not documented in the standard sea lion texts I have read. What I've learned directly from their behavior has changed what I know, how I care for them, and how I train new zookeepers.

I am sad to say that there is a tremendous amount of garbage and other pollutants in our oceans today. Plastic was developed a little over one hundred years ago; sea lions evolved thousands of years ago and they didn't have to contend with modern contaminants until relatively recently. Many animals, not only California sea lions and their pups, get confused and will consume balloons, plastic, and soda can snap tabs, virtually anything floating. California sea lions, as I've said, are opportunistic eaters. They eat quickly as they swim, sometimes ingesting trash like it is squid or a school of fish. Sea lions will swim into schools of fish and may consume pounds of them at a time. A plastic bag underwater may look like squid. A deflated balloon could look like a mackerel or herring. Cigarette butts may resemble tiny fish. When you are a hungry sea lion and eating quickly, consuming garbage is common. We don't know if sea lions will become selective eaters and stop being the opportunists that they have evolved to be. I want to hope they do, but I doubt they will.

Every Day Is a Gift

A few years ago, I volunteered at the sea lion rescue center in California that saved Star and Angel's lives. At this visit, I donated to them a portion of the proceeds from the sale of my first book, *Puff the Sea Lion: A Love Story*. I wanted something good to come from Puff's unexpected death and it has. To this day, the money from the sale of the book benefits wild sea lions and a local program that my friend runs for the underprivileged who cannot afford to spay or neuter their pet dogs and cats. While at the center, I saw sea lions with fishing line and other debris cutting into their necks; there were animals with throats and digestive systems stuffed with plastic bags, cigarette butts, drinking straws, and balloon strings. Some were missing eyes, had open wounds, or were starving.

Disease is always a tremendous threat to weak, sick, and injured animals. We had to guard against many serious diseases such as brucellosis. Every time we entered or exited the rehabilitation enclosures, which was under quarantine at all times, we had to disinfect our shoes and the protective yellow, rubber coveralls we always wore while working with the animals. I am very used to communicating with the animals I work with at the zoo, giving tender words of encouragement throughout the day. Protocol at the rescue center is to keep these wild animals wild. They need to remain fearful of people so they avoid contact with humans when they encounter them. I understood immediately what my tasks at the center were and keeping these animals separate from humans was imperative.

The duties of a sea lion rescuer are similar to the responsibilities of a zookeeper who cares for sea lions. We both meet the animals' basic needs: providing a clean and safe place for the animal to thrive, clean water in which to swim, and quality fish to eat. At the same time, it is different because a zoo is a permanent home where animal/human bonds are created to benefit the animal's quality of life. At a rescue center, these bonds are exactly what wild sea lions do *not* need. It would not benefit these animals if they approached humans in the wild because they remembered humans were friendly to them. That would encourage them to approach humans, and human contact is not safe. You'll recall that Star and Angel were shot. Bullets only come from humans.

When I fed the animals at the center, we went in with 4-foot by 3-foot plastic boards to keep the sea lions fearful of us; we tossed the fish around quickly, never speaking. We made sure each animal received the appropriate amount of fish, but we didn't linger. Feeding was quick and efficient so the animals would not associate humans with food. This method was effective. The animals did not imprint on humans and that was one of the rescue center's many goals.

My visit to the marine mammal care center enlightened me in many ways. I always felt fortunate to have Star and Angel in my life, but after looking at hundreds of extremely ill animals that would not have survived without our intervention made me want to go back to work and just gaze at Star, Angel, and PJ, a little longer than I usually did, with more gratitude than I usually had.

Meanwhile we continued the long process of weaning PJ. He was long past the time other sea lions his age would have started eating fish. For weeks we had been offering him cut up fish like the other sea lions consumed as their daily diet. We'd offered fish like this many times to him in the past, but for some reason he did not think fish was food. I called an expert on sea lion pup weaning. He told me an animal that is not hungry will not eat and a healthy animal would not let itself starve. I was so concerned because the little butterball was shrinking; I felt better after hearing this.

I consulted other sea lion caregivers from around the nation and they gave me some ideas to aid in this weaning process. One professional suggested to me that we separate PJ from his mother if possible. However, we didn't have a separate area to take PJ.

59

Another person said to tie a fish on a string and run around activating his prey drive. Feeling like a fool, but hoping he would follow the fish and eat it, I ran around with a fish tied to a string. PJ chased the fish and I almost tripped and fell into the pool, but I would do whatever was needed. PJ enjoyed this game and thought I was great, but strange.

I was also told live minnows should do the trick and another person I consulted said to freeze pieces of fish in ice cube trays. We tried each and every idea to get this little guy interested in fish, but PJ still chose not to eat and was still losing weight; he was down to just fifty-five pounds.

The next step would be to do an assisted feed, to actually put fish in his mouth and make him swallow. We really didn't want to have to do that. It would be stressful on all of us, especially if we had to do it more than once. Sea lions are eating garbage in the ocean and PJ won't eat nutritious fish. SERIOUSLY?

The vet staff came in to see what could be done with PJ. One of the staff, sat on the floor with PJ for over an hour sliding fish ice cubes back and forth. Finally, thank God, PJ ate one, then two, then three! The next day I brought in a cake with a picture of a mackerel on it for the sea lion staff to eat and we celebrated. That day PJ ate a pound of capelin and mackerel cut into little pieces and we all took a deep breath. Next, we needed to get his weight back up to the butterball mark and then begin his husbandry training.

Within a year, PJ gained over one hundred pounds and learned forty different behaviors! PJ was intelligent just like his parents Star and Puff; genetically he had brains and brawn. He trusted me unconditionally and I taught him using the rules of positive reinforcement, adding praise, hugs, and soothing petting as secondary reinforcers. He called to me for food and I would come. I would summon him to a training session and he would stop what he was doing and quickly meet me. He would come to me, no questions asked, ready for our next game, similar to how he and his mother communicated before feedings.

Sometimes when I entered the inside holding room to clean it, PJ would bound in with a toy in his mouth tossing it back and forth. He would look around the corner at me then dive in the pool. He wanted me to play. I stopped my work, of course, to see what he had in mind. We would play with the toy he brought in or I would take my shoes off and walk around the shallow pool he was swimming in. The ends of my shorts would get wet while I was petting him and he was swimming between my legs. How I loved his father Puff, and boy did we have fun, but Puff had never invited me into the water or perhaps I didn't notice things then like I do now. Every sea lion I have worked with has opened my eyes a little more to the realm of sea lion behavior and communication. I have worked with eleven different sea lions in thirty years. Each taught me that sea lions are distinct individuals, with unique personalities and all learned best when trained with love and understanding. PJ made little clicks and chirps while we were in the water together. In all my research on them, I had never read that California sea lions communicate this way. I was amazed at the time and now as I think back to those precious moments I smile and my heart fills with joy.

I hope other zookeepers give the animals in their care the play time they need and discover what I have learned. This is the difference between what people consider a job and a lifelong career that is their life's passion. The relationships with the animals make you accept a job where you are underpaid (less than $12.00 an hour starting wages where I am employed) and where you have to work the weekends and holidays losing time with family and friends. Why? Because strangely enough, the animals become part of your family and friends as well.

Puff used to make the noises PJ was making when we played at the gallery glass. He would be in the outside pool underwater and I would be on the other side of the glass in the Rocky Coasts gallery. When all was quiet, I could hear Puff make these gentle noises when he saw me, especially the first thing in the morning. I know that when I responded with a perky "Good morning, big buddy" to his little clicks and squeaks he could hear me because I could hear his greeting. His eyes would light up and he would squeak again. A year after Puff's death, I was now here in the water with PJ. I never could have imagined ever playing in the water with Puff's son. I knew this moment was a gift from God—so precious that I will keep it with my greatest life memories.

One game I taught PJ was to put his toys into a recycling bin. I would get very creative hiding his toys in the water and on land. PJ would have to locate them, pick them up with his mouth, and then drop the toys into the bin. He loved this game; he was always up for the challenge. I was as excited as he was as I watched his eyes light up while in search of a toy, his little body hopping up on land or diving underwater, looking for a particular one. When he succeeded, he could not wait for the game to start again and neither could I. Every time we are with an animal, or human for that matter, we add to the relationship, take away from the relationship, or have a neutral encounter. That is how training works and how relationships are built. Every time I played at the gallery glass, or when I went out into their habitat to give them a toy, hose, or ice to play with, or when I fed them and spoke encouraging words to them, I increased the trust between us and built up our relationship. If I were to accidently trip and fall on them, that would be a negative influence. Some trainers use punishment in their training practice. This does not create life-long bonds. It destroys trust and relationships. When my children were born, I answered their cries, sang to them, read to them, hugged them tight with kisses. If I were to lie to them or yell at them or belittle them it would diminish our relationship. I was honest and gentle with my boys and we have a loving relationship even now that they are full grown. It's how I treat the animals in my care as well.

California sea lions are used in our armed forces to keep our nation safe. They are trained to find objects underwater that human divers are unable to locate. Sea lions can swim 25 miles an hour and dive over 800 feet in the ocean depths, faster and deeper than any human is able. I met a woman at the marine mammal rescue center who was volunteering there the same time as I. I was very interested to learn that she trained a California sea lion to put a hook on a designated item within the oceans' depths. She went out into the open ocean with this sea lion, to which she became much attached, and trained him to find and, if necessary, remove various military objects. I am always astonished by what an animal can accomplish when properly trained. Finally, to meet someone who has a career I have only read about and then hear of her relationship with an animal and their successes, opens my mind to all the things that are happening every day around us because of animal training. I have learned more about myself by asking questions, volunteering when I felt it in my heart it was a worthwhile cause, and through observation. Taking the opportunity to leave my comfort zone and ask others about their experiences often taught me more than a book or thesis might; life experiences can be amazing and life changing. As much as I love to read, volunteering to actually do something gives me a different perspective. The people and places encountered, the sights, sounds and personalities experienced during a volunteer event, add to my knowledge in a way books cannot.

Puff and Flounder were the best retrievers I ever met. Because of their size and strength, they could pick up large toys filled with water and bring them to me. One day I gave them a five-gallon plastic watercooler bottle filled with fish; at first these containers floated. Flounder and Puff would push the jug on top of the water, looking through the clear plastic trying to solve the riddle of getting the fish into their mouths. Eventually they figured out they had to tip the container and fill it with water, which would raise the fish to the narrow neck of the bottle allowing them to pluck the fish out from the only opening.

After all the fish were eaten, I would find the containers filled with water at the bottom of the pool. I knew retrieving them would be a challenge for the two sea lions because there were no handles; when filled with water, this plastic container weighed approximately forty pounds. The current from the filter system complicated the task further. I have noticed when you work with intelligent animals (this includes humans) learning really begins when you present them with a challenge. I knew the bottles were heavy and awkward to bring to the surface. I asked Flounder to get a jug. He didn't rush to get it; he went about fetching every other toy instead. I gave him a fish for each toy he brought to me because I wanted him to continue until I could see if he could understand and accomplish the task of retrieving the jug. If I discontinued reinforcing Flounder when he retrieved his toys, he might not feel inclined to get to that last challenging item.

I had toys all around me on the beach and then it was just me, Flounder, and that very heavy jug at the bottom of the pool. I was hopeful that he would do it because we liked "picking-up" after ourselves together. This was a behavior with a high reinforcement history. I gave him the retrieval signal. He searched the pool until he touched the only toy left in the pool. I clicked my clicker. Flounder could hear this sound underwater and he then knew the precise moment I was communicating with him. He looked up at me from deep in the pool and I gave him a little extra motivation. I raised my arms up over my head with a big smile on my face while jumping up and down. I had taught Flounder to fetch 17 years before this. He knew by my actions that he was on the right track. I ran to some stairs that are on the outdoor sea lion habitat to assist him succeeding with this task. Slowly he pushed that container from the bottom of the pool to me. I was lying on my stomach, arms extended, chanting, "You can do it; you can do it." As Flounder swam towards me, I could see his eyes were focused in deep concentration. (Boy, do I miss him.) The jug was in my grasp in moments. I emptied the water out of it and tossed it on land while praising that good boy. I threw many fish straight up in the air and as they landed into the pool, I yelled, "GOOD BOY!" Flounder always liked a new game because it was always fun. I made sure it was.

Star was another exceptional toy recycler, but because of the loss of her left eye her perception was skewed. That did not stop her from trying harder and she never gave up! I would be sitting with the recycling bin and Star would slide up with a toy in her mouth and then line it up with the blue bin that was in front of me and release the toy. If the toy hit the lip of the bin and did not make it in, Star would chase the toy, put it in her mouth and try again and I would cheer her on. At times, one of my colleagues and I began speaking in "pirate" when Star entered a room. Her only eye would be moving around doing the work of two and her sweet head would be tilting this way and that accessing the situation around her. She was strong, smart and brave, like a fictional pirate. "Aye, I be wanting some fishies" we would say lovingly, when she comically slid inside to start a training session. She filled the room with her presence and intelligence. Other trainers nicknamed her, "Sea Star and Superstar" because she touched their hearts and amazed them as well.

Years ago, I began desensitizing the sea lions in my care to a plastic tray that held medical equipment such as a stethoscope, empty syringe, thermometer, flashlight, and toothbrush. Initially the animals were afraid of anything new. Being touched by a foreign object took extra desensitizing. These animals taught me that when you have a relationship with them, making many positive memories, they will trust you until the end. This is the truth.

One of my favorite memories of PJ involved this medical tray. As part of the summer sea lion demonstrations, I usually give the sea lions a physical; we quickly go through the medical exam using the items in the tray. This enlightens our guests on how well we care for our animals and the process that we use to get them comfortable in participating in their own health care. During one of the exams, I had just given Star a mock injection, a mock blood draw, checked her heart, checked her eyes, and took a mock temperature. She and I moved off to another area to do the recycling bin routine. This was another message we shared with our guests: the importance of recycling and keeping our oceans clean. While Star and I were busy conveying this message to our zoo patrons, PJ was busy as well. I had left the tray of medical tools on the beach and of course PJ assumed it was for his enjoyment. While I am training animals, I am commonly oblivious to outside distractions. Most times I am in my own world focused on each movement or subtle response from the animal I am working with. This time was different. I heard human laughter all around me. Sweet little PJ had pulled the tray of medical supplies from the beach into the water. This 12-inch by 6-inch plastic "boat" was floating in the pool; why it did not sink or lose its contents, I don't know. All I saw was PJ playfully whipping the stethoscope in his mouth from right to left. I could actually hear it smack his body, while hearing people say how cute he was and laughing at his playfulness. I thought it was funny too, but I did not want PJ to accidently ingest any of the items or have them get stuck in the filter system. I asked Star to be my hero. She gently pushed the tray through the water to me while I waited on land on my hands and knees, my right arm extended, cheering her on. Then I managed to get the stethoscope away from a very active pup playing a game of keep-away with his foolish human, namely me.

Chapter 5
From Pup to Bull,
PJ Matures

PJ at almost three, weighing 180 pounds

Because I knew he would most likely be sent to another zoo when he got older, I made every day with PJ count. I could not wait to go to work and spend time with him. I wanted to shape a gentle, respectful sea lion, one everyone would like to work with.

As a zoo animal, he would be communicating and working with people for the rest of his life. I hoped his new people would be understanding and fun and that they would learn to love him as much as I did. I needed his future to be bright for my heart to stay whole. Joy and fun filled our days. PJ allowed me to weigh him, touch him, and examine every inch of his body. This meant we could take care of him if he became ill. I wouldn't have changed a thing, but PJ was getting older. If allowed, he would breed with his mother when he matured. We needed to make a decision on what to do. The choices were to neuter him, to give him medicine to suppress his hormones, put his mother on birth control, separate him from his mother (because on occasion sea lions in human care will breed out of season), or we would have to find PJ a new home at another zoo. The zoo's administration chose to ship PJ to another zoo. Although a couple of accredited zoos were initially interested in housing a quickly growing bull sea lion, for one reason or another they changed their minds.

Meanwhile, PJ was becoming sexually mature; he would turn two on June 1. June is the most active month for California sea lions as it marks the peak of the birthing/breeding season. Whether in a zoo or on the California beaches this is true. In the ocean, the largest, strongest male sea lions become the beach masters. After bulking up in preparation for mating season, these males can weigh up to 900 pounds. After gaining this weight, they can fast up to 100 days. This enables them to fight for and retain up to seventeen of the most fertile females and defend the most sought-after beach property without being inconvenienced by the need to eat.

PJ was beginning to act like an adolescent male sea lion, not a pup anymore. He was the only male sea lion at our zoo at the time so he was beach master. I was informed by another sea lion expert at a conference I attended that at their facility a one-year old bull pup impregnated their 29-year-old cow/female sea lion. The cow was kept solitary to ensure she didn't become pregnant. Their administration thought a pup could keep her company because sea lions are social animals. She became pregnant and I was told the pup was born healthy.

I was concerned because PJ was territorial, barking, and trying as hard as he could to herd and corral Star and Angel. For hours, he would practice trying to push them off the beach. Puff, PJ's father, weighed four-hundred pounds when he was four years old. PJ had a lot of eating and growing to do to equal that; he weighed about 180 pounds at the time. Star and Angel weighed about 200 pounds each. It was a close match size–wise, but PJ was no match for these ladies when it came to agility and beach smarts. Star, that one-eyed sea lion, still not considered a full-grown adult at 5 years old, was an excellent mother. She would not let him win. She would pin him down with her neck and push him in the pool repeatedly. Star was teaching him how to be a bull sea lion. Star was always a tomboy. It would not help him at all if she let him win. If PJ were ever to meet another male sea lion, he probably would put up a fight for territory, a natural behavior. I watched Star teaching PJ day after day. During these days they were exerting an immense amount of energy and consequently were extremely hungry. They each would eat almost twenty-five pounds of fish every day and still be hungry.

I recall one of their wrestling sessions clearly. It looked to me as if PJ was getting the better of Star. Their necks were pushing at each other using all their body weight and they were both breathing heavily. Each would push the other with all their might to get the other to fall in the pool. This went on for well over an hour and for one second it looked like Star was going to fall in the water. It would have been the first time I witnessed PJ winning over Star, however, at just the right moment sweet, little Angel jumped up on the rock next to her best friend, Star, and pushed PJ into the water. Yay! Girl power!

PJ thought that was great and wanted an instant replay! Angel and Star had a different idea. With their tail ends together on one end and their mouths open on the other, they both stretched out over the rock taking over the prime real estate. PJ tried to attack from the water, but he did not get anywhere. Even without knowing much about sea lions, the zoo guests who were watching recognized what they were seeing and a few cheered when PJ plunked in the water. No one should push their mother around even if you are a sea lion.

Chapter 6
Welcome to the Family, Hut!

Hut's first day

Right around this time our zoo agreed to bring another sea lion to live with our little sea lion family, a nine-year old bull named Hut. Of course, there is a story behind his name. As a pup he washed up on the California coast where he was rehabilitated and released a number of times only to wash up on shore again. He was found in a hut used by the local fishermen. He was ultimately deemed non-releasable by the rescue center's veterinarians because of his inability to stay in the ocean. He found a good home with loving people away from the ocean in an aquarium setting. His life served as a way to share important messages: that sea lions are beautiful animals; that they learn easily with positive reinforcement; and that our oceans are not the fresh ecosystems they were before humans began polluting them. In the near future, zoos may be the only place on earth wild animals are safe due to not only pollution of our air and water, but also deforestation, illegal hunting, poaching, and human over-population and encroachment on wild habitats. Our world is losing animals in nature at an alarming rate. It appears half of humanity seeks to destroy animals and nature while the rest of us strive to conserve the resources on earth and save its inhabitants. We may be the only species left in a destroyed world if we are not careful. We must act now and persistently.

An aquarium had been Hut's home for more than nine years and the people and other animals there were his family. SSP (Species Survival Plan) had selected our zoo to be a breeding facility for California sea lions. Angel, Star and Hut were all born on the California beaches. Their bloodlines were chosen by SSP to help diversify the genetics of the California sea lion in America's zoos.

I was asked by my supervisors to travel to Hut's home to meet him and see how he was trained and how he lived. I would then accompany him home to our zoo. The knowledge I gained would make Hut's transition to our zoo easier for him and our staff.

I remember clearly taking care of Angel, Star and PJ the last day it was just the three of them. Our system and daily routine went flawlessly. They knew what to expect from their trainers and we enjoyed teaching them and watching them play. They played all day, especially games of tag and keep-away. They were the most active, playful, and healthy animals you could imagine. I knew things would change with our new addition and I was hoping all would be fine and that Hut would soon be playing with this high energy group of pinnipeds.

I traveled to Hut's home as arranged and met the people who loved him and who had taught him many behaviors. Hut was beautiful; he had an adorable pup like face and his coat was shiny and smooth. But it was his demeanor that really had me speechless. He was absolutely the calmest sea lion I had ever met. After I was trained by Hut's caregivers on how to care for him, they asked me to go through some of his exercises with him. He looked up at me with the warmest and most intelligent gaze, waited for my request, completed it faultlessly, and then quietly waited for another request. His trainers told me his likes and dislikes and that I could contact them anytime if we had any questions.

Hut entered the transport crate perfectly. The crate was loaded on the back of an enclosed trailer. His trainer and I sat with him in the back of the truck as it bounced down the road. After a while a camera was added so we could watch him while we were in the driver's cabin. We stopped often to check on him. I am sure he could not wait to arrive at his new home and neither could I. We arrived safe and sound. A front-end loader lifted and carried his crate to a pickup truck which took him to the sea lion area. PJ, Star, and Angel were locked outside on the beach while this process was taking place. When the crate was opened, Hut slipped right out of the crate and into the water of the inside pool. Good boy! We were going to do everything we could to make him feel at home. I was hopeful he would get along with the others. They were a hectic bunch and he seemed so calm. Only time would tell.

It is our zoo's policy when animals arrive to keep them on quarantine for a month to make sure they are healthy and have those thirty days to adjust to their new surroundings. Hut's trainer, who knew his normal behavior, told us Hut was not acting like himself while he was alone in our inside holding room. I watched him as he lay flat on the floor with a distant look in his eyes. I have worked with sea lions for thirty years and the only time I have seen this behavior was when an animal was resting before or after falling asleep. This was not the case with Hut. Our vet staff did an assessment and decided that to benefit Hut's mental health, he could meet our motley crew of sea lions through the fencing sooner rather than later. Physically he passed two veterinary exams with flying colors, but he needed a little social interaction and our charges, Star, Angel, and PJ, were just what the doctor ordered. We opened the door to the outside area and Star, smart and adventurous sea lion that she was, came in first, of course. As I watched, Star zipped in, peeked through the fencing with her one eye at Hut, then slid back outside. Soon Angel came in and made a similar introduction and then left as well. While staying outside, PJ cautiously peeked inside. PJ had been the only male sea lion at our zoo before Hut's arrival, therefore, by default, he was the dominate male; in his mind, this was his pool and Star and Angel made up his harem. Considering that hormones are the driving force in an adolescent mammal, I thought to myself, "We may have some concerns during this introduction."

We decided to introduce Hut to the others before the month-long quarantine was over; he acted as if he wanted to be with the others. When Star slid into the holding room to look at the newcomer through the fence, Hut would dip his head in and out of the water while floating in the holding area pool acknowledging Star's arrival. "Adorable," I thought to myself, "how inviting." I understood that this was an "I want to play" gesture even though I had never witnessed it before. Star would bound out of the holding area, only to quickly return to pick up a rubber floor mat that came with Hut. She had never seen this type of "toy" before. She picked it up with her mouth and wiggled it at the gate that separated her and Hut, all the while looking directly at him. Star was definitely trying to be intriguing, and certainly not playing "hard to get." I was having fun watching these two strangers communicate through body language.

How animals communicate with each other is fascinating and we really don't know enough about it. This is one of the most interesting parts of my job, witnessing the relationships the animals choose to forge with each other. Some just tolerate one another and others develop strong bonds. It is their choice; we, their humans, cannot make this choice for them. They decide who will be their friend or not.

We soon received approval for Hut to fully meet his new sea lion family. We opened the door from the inside pool and he slid to the outside door to take a look around. Star and Angel met him at the opening from the beach side. Hut was on a lower level of rock work when he entered the outside habitat. This meant Star and Angel had the upper rocks and by approaching Hut at a higher level it would make them appear larger than they were and possibly more dominant. Star looked at him with interest. Angel, however, met him with an open mouth and a straight neck pointed at him, a defensive posture. Normally, Angel was shy. It was interesting to witness Angel protecting her pool and her family. I was surprised, then happy for her, because she felt powerful enough to protect her home from an intruder. She was showing her own independence.

Then I saw Hut's expression and posture and I felt pity. Poor, Buddy! He had left his aquarium family to become part of this one and Angel was not being welcoming. I walked out on to the beach about one hundred feet away from Hut and I called Angel to me. She swam over and quickly jumped up next to me then turned her head towards our new bull to glare at him. I began petting Angel and in soothing tones, I told her, "Be nice. Everything will be okay." I hoped she understood me. I realized she was doing what she thought she had to. Hut's trainer, the one who came with him from his old home, walked out onto the beach with him. She was talking sweetly to him, encouraging him to be brave. He jumped into the water and we cheered. There was zoo staff standing above the water at several different positions observing the introduction. I decided to get a different view and left the beach for the Rocky Coasts gallery to observe them all underwater. I would be able to see clearer from there if we needed to intervene and separate them.

When I arrived in the gallery, I saw Hut lying on the bottom of the pool being as still as he possibly could be. Angel and Star repeatedly darted underwater with their mouths open, swam very close to him, and then at the last second veered away from him. Star and Angel were working to keep their home safe and to tell this newcomer that they were in charge. They were both smaller and had permanent injuries from bullet wounds. Here we thought they would need protecting, but it was Hut who was the underdog. He was so gentle; he never thought to act aggressively even to protect himself from these imps. I was beginning to really like this guy! PJ quietly kept his distance and let the ladies drive the message home to Hut.

Soon they relented and Hut began swimming around. PJ, Star, and Angel began playing among themselves as usual and Hut kept to himself. All in all, the introduction went well. I only wished they would all play together, but this was only the first few minutes of day one. I said to myself, "One day at a time."

The next day PJ showed interest in Hut by riding on his back. This is usually a submissive behavior, but PJ was wrapping his flippers around Hut's midsection. PJ was actually trying to dominate this male who was eight years older and one hundred and seventy pounds heavier. Hut didn't seem to care or he didn't know what PJ was doing. Both PJ and I knew what PJ was doing. It took a few weeks before they began really playing with each other. I was so thrilled when I saw them holding each other's tail and going around and around underwater in a friendly spin. I watched, smiling, until I was giddy. They were developing a positive relationship and for this I was extremely grateful. We have a duty to give the animals in our care the best life possible. They absolutely deserve happiness.

76

Chapter 7
Every Day Is a Gift

Spending time with Angel

One morning in the early summer of 2015, Star came inside for her morning exam and training session. She appeared to be confused. I couldn't tell if she was having vision problems, but she was clearly disorientated. I offered her a fish, but she acted distracted and then surprised to see me there. For years Star's routine was to come inside before every feeding. She was not here out of morning hunger that was for sure. I was concerned and began to wonder if the shrapnel in her head was causing this confusion. I always compared Star to a cartoon character with her crazy antics. She was always fun and ready to learn, but she was not acting that way now. Zookeepers are advocates for the animals in their care. We know them best. It is our duty to convey our concerns to the vet if we see a change in behavior.

I radioed our vet staff and shared my observations and concerns. They told me to keep an eye on her and notify them of any changes. They suggested when she started feeling better that we should x-ray her head to see if anything was apparent that would cause her confusion. Positive reinforcement training is fantastic. However, when an animal is not hungry, is ill, or is confused like Star was that day, the animal may not participate. They may not understand what we want from them when they are ill. During the next training session, Star ate some fish, but still was not herself. However, it was an improvement and I told the vet staff. By the end of the day I felt good that Star was eating and participating, not as eagerly as usual, but nonetheless her appetite and activity level was better. My weekend was about to begin, but I was confident that Star was in good hands. Our team communicated well with one another

I was about to face a challenge on the home front. The next morning my father called me, saying my mom was not making sense. He tried to put her on the phone. All I could hear was pained mumbling. I told my dad that if he didn't call 911, I would. He said he would call. I live about 7 miles from my parents' house. I drove over there right away and arrived just in time to see my mother being put in an ambulance. I followed her to the hospital. She didn't know who she was or where she was. The doctors asked how long she had been this way. I think they thought she had dementia. I told them she mowed her lawn, paid the bills, and was my father's caregiver. For fifty-four days my mom was hospitalized with kidney failure brought on by a urinary tract infection and huge kidney stones, called staghorn stones because they imbed into the kidney and can fill it entirely like with my mother. My mother only has one kidney; she had lost the other kidney to cancer two years previously. When Mom was brought to the hospital, we all met in emergency. The doctors asked my father if they should resuscitate the love of his life. I looked over at my frail father sitting in a wheelchair and watched him somberly nod. Mom was in ICU for weeks. I held her hand and prayed for her and with her every day. My mom didn't talk for days, just some mumbling through the pain. I held her hand and I felt peace. In my heart, I said to God it was okay for Mom to go. I would do my best to take care of Dad. Everyone has their time. I prayed for the peace of Jesus to wash over us. I felt the love I had for my mother and God's love for us.

The room was dark and quiet, like it had been for hours each day, the only sound the beeping of many machines monitoring her. After a few moments, my mom began speaking frantically. She said, "Dear God, Dear God," over and over for several minutes. These were the first words she had spoken in a long time. I was not sure what was going on. Then I understood. My mom was calling the Lord. She opened her eyes and looked straight ahead and then said, "Look at the light." Like a small child she said, "Oh, hi God," like one would say to a dear friend that she was not expecting. Then she said, "Hey, where are you going?" Then all was quiet. Mom relaxed and started breathing normally. She lived, and although she doesn't remember much of her stay at the hospital, she remembered this incident. God reminded my mother and me that He is with us. I stayed and prayed with her every day for 54 days until it was time for her to go home. The day I prayed that I was ready to let her go didn't change the outcome. It was not up to me. The only thing up to me was how I handled things. I went into the hospital every day, put a smile on my face, and told my mom I loved her whether she was awake to hear me or not. I would talk to the doctors and nurses about my mother's condition, then cry all the way home.

During my mother's illness, Star was on my mind as well. The animals at the zoo are my family too. I advocate for them as well as for my human family. I am with them during the good times and bad. I celebrate holidays with them because zookeepers work weekends and holidays. I shovel paths for them when it snows and feed them nutritious food. I think about how I can make their lives better every day. The way I feel about them is hard to describe. They heal me when I am weary. They deserve everything I can give them because of what they have given me.

After being in the hospital those first initial trying days, I could not wait to see how Star was feeling. I had not received a call from work (no news is good news). When I returned to work, I saw Star was back to her old silly self. Yay! But now Angel was unwell. When I came in that morning, I was told that Angel was sleeping alone inside, barking at any sea lion that tried to lay with her, and not eating. It was June, breeding and birthing season for the California sea lion.

Angel was six years old at the time and had never had a pup. Our new bull, Hut, of course, had been with us since May, but Angel was keeping to herself and this is not typical breeding behavior. I thought perhaps she was in false labor similar to what she experienced in 2013 when PJ was born. She kept to herself and held her abdomen. The vet staff had been notified days ago and left instructions to alert them of any changes. PJ was two years old. Was it possible Angel and PJ bred last year when PJ was one? Gestation is one year, a nine-month pregnancy with a three-month delayed implantation. I contacted other sea lion experts around the country. They thought it could be a pregnancy issue because of the time of year it was. All I knew is Angel had better start eating, it had been too long.

On day six of her illness, I saw her perk up a little when I came in the room. I started talking to her sweetly, positively, encouraging her just like I did every day. I began tossing fish in Angel's inside pool. "Go get them, Angel," I said. She sat up and looked at the pool for the first time in days. "Good girl! You'll never catch them," I said tossing the fish back and forth in the pool. I tried to sound thrilled when in fact I was entirely too concerned to feel any resemblance of joy. Angel slowly slid in the pool and took a fish in her mouth and started chewing it. "GOOD GIRL! GET THEM, ANGEL!" I cheered her on. She ate two pounds of fish that morning and she let me pet her. Needless to say, I did not want to lose her. At the next feeding, she went on the scale when I asked and she weighed 176 lbs. She had lost 18 pounds. I told the vet staff she ate two pounds of fish and we were all happy that she was feeling better. I saw her getting stronger every day and I was very grateful.

After work, I would visit my mother in the hospital. I also had two teenage sons who needed a mother's love and advice. My husband was by my side and I am sure I wasn't the partner he deserved. And there were three dogs and a cat that needed my love and attention as well. My mother and Angel did not need to know how worried I was about each of them.

Just as Angel's situation was improving that day, my Dad called me at work and told me my mom had had a stroke at the nursing home during her rehabilitation. She was in the hospital again. My coworkers hugged me and told me they would finish my assignments for the day and not to worry about the animals. I said a quick prayer as I rushed to leave work to visit Mom. The doctors caught the stroke quickly. That was very good news. Mom's right side was not functioning and she was having trouble speaking and swallowing. Soon a feeding tube was put in so she would not aspirate. I left the hospital late that night making sure my Dad got home safely. My Dad had been in ill-health for a number of years with several aliments, including congestive heart failure that made him extremely weak and caused him to fall frequently. Now, he was tired after spending all day at the hospital and I did not want him to fall in the driveway or in the house.

Then at work there was a new complication with the sea lions. PJ had not entirely enjoyed the arrival of Hut to his pool or in his life for that matter. He was old enough to breed, but now Angel and Star were behaving differently and showing more interest in Hut. Hut was sleeping with Star and Angel in PJ's spot. I would find PJ swimming alone outside because Hut chased him away from Star and Angel. He did not know when or where to relax and he was playing less. He and Hut were engaging in natural displacement behavior and Hut was becoming the dominant male.

Already disconcerted by Hut's arrival, PJ appeared confused by the new staffing. Five additional people were added to the sea lion staff. None of the sea lions were familiar with these new keepers. He played with Hut at times, but because this was breeding season his demeanor changed. I could feel his anxiety. I understood it was the breeding season's raging youth hormones. The formerly fun little guy began moving around and swimming quickly with big wide eyes.

Each sea lion has a different personality and I love them all the same for different reasons. Angel enjoys quiet, calm training sessions, where Star is sharp and quick to learn or she will invent a new game with me or a sea lion friend. I had spent a lot of time with PJ teaching him manners, how to be patient during training, and to be gentle when he received his fish. I knew he would be learning behaviors from people for the rest of his life. At this very young age, PJ knew over forty behaviors that we had taught him. I accepted this role as teacher/trainer very seriously because PJ's future was in the balance. Now it was all I could do to keep him focused. It takes time to teach behaviors to an animal and patience and understanding.

Every morning when I awoke, I would thank God for all His blessings. I thought of all the things I was grateful for and I would acknowledge that I am God's servant and that I love these animals in His name. No one said it would be easy. I prayed for strength, wisdom, and understanding.

On the home front, things were much better. My mom was home! My dad became her caregiver. The tables were turned in my parents' marriage and they embraced their second (or was this their third?) chance at life together. Now that is love! They celebrated life everyday as we all should, treating every day as a gift.

Soon after my mother's miraculous return home, Hut became ill. One afternoon, he refused his last feeding and laid outside on the rock embankment, just looking at me. Male sea lions fast during the breeding season, but breeding season was almost over and he did not act like this earlier in the summer. The fact is every animal reacts differently throughout the seasons because each is an individual and of course each circumstance has variables. The next morning, I was hoping Hut would be back to his usual self.

First thing the next morning we entered the sea lion holding area. Hut was beached inside lying in a strange position. I said, "Hey, Buddy, are you okay?" He tried to move but his right side was not responding correctly. We observed his locomotion to better understand what was going on and to evaluate his health. He jostled about and began moving; his mobility was definitely impaired. He went outside. I noticed his eyes had a strange look to them and his jaw began to open and close for no reason. Once he was in the water, it appeared he was having seizures.

We had to drain the 100,000-gallon pool as quickly as possible or he would drown. I called Star, Angel and PJ back inside so they could be locked in the holding rooms and be safe. We could not drain the pool with them out there. One of them was bound to get injured if the pool was empty. Despite all the chaos, they came right inside when asked, proving again that training saves lives for sure!

Positive reinforcement training saves lives, but as I've said sometimes animals are too ill to participate. It appeared Hut could hear us, but his body wasn't doing what he wanted it to do. He knew his name. I knew this because he looked in my direction, albeit with unfocused eyes, when I called him. He tried to get out of the pool several times unsuccessfully. Whatever was wrong with him was restricting his physical and mental abilities. The vet staff stood ready to tranquilize him for an exam once the pool was drained. Again, if he was tranquilized in the water he could drown, so draining the pool was imperative.

Hut was looking around with big eyes and his jaw was clapping. Zoo staff was on the beach just in case we had to dive in to keep his head above water until the pool emptied. We had never seen anything like this. It seemed like the pool took forever to drain. We were all on edge not knowing what would happen next. Thankfully, in a matter of minutes, Hut was resting in just a few inches of water. The vet staff darted him with tranquilizers. We placed him in a cargo net and carried him to the inside holding area where we could obtain a blood sample and give him a thorough physical. The blood samples would be sent out to labs for analysis. We all had questions about his condition and were very concerned.

The aquatic life support staff immediately began re-filling the pool so the other sea lions could safely go outside. Hut needed to be alone inside to recuperate without the danger of water or a pool. Next, we had to see how he acted when he woke up from being tranquilized. He did wake up, thank God. As we evaluated him, we concluded he still did not have control of his body.

Every Day Is a Gift

For days, we kept him alone and quiet following the orders of our zoo veterinarian. I would go into the holding room to offer him food and find him lying still. I would have to tap him several times or even shake him to wake him up to make sure he was alive. This does not happen with a healthy sea lion; we do not have to physically wake them. We knew at any moment Hut's health could change for the better or worse. We zookeepers became a stronger team because of our love for him and our determination to get him through this. He did not eat for two days, did not even try to eat. I watched him day after day just lay there near the inside holding pool. I didn't know what to think, but I knew what to do; I kept praying for him.

Caring for my parents provided me with the insight to understand what I needed to do. There were many similarities with Hut. When at various times my dad and most recently my mom were in the hospital for a very long time, I visited them every day to cheer them up and be their advocate. I knew how to pretend all was well, when in all honesty I really was never sure. I acted this way with Hut. I came in offering him food like he wasn't ill. "Let's go," I would say. I would blow his whistle to start a training session. On day three he tried to eat. I would pet him and tell him what a good boy he was and that he was doing great. He could not swallow or vocalize. On day four his eating attempts increased but he started chewing his fish. Sea lions don't chew their fish. Their teeth are designed for ripping and tearing and they usually swallow their fish whole. Nevertheless, this indicated improvement. His mouth was beginning to work!

Weeks went by and he slowly began moving without falling over. We saw further small signs of recovery each day. He had excellent care from the veterinary staff and his zookeepers. Soon he was gaining weight and we put him back with his sea lion family. Then we received the astonishing results of the bloodwork. He had contracted a mosquito-borne illness, Eastern Equine

Encephalitis. Hut was documented as the first California sea lion to be treated for this illness and survive.

I have never been to medical school so this is only from my observations and my thirty years of zoo animal experience; looking back to the weeks prior to Hut's illness when Star was confused and Angel did not eat for six days, it makes me think Hut may not have been the first survivor or the only survivor of EEE, but we will never know for certain.

Chapter 8
A New Home for PJ

The winter of 2015 was bitterly cold. As the temperatures plunged, the sea lions' appetites increased. Living in a climate like New York's, in order to endure the weather in and out of the water, the sea lions eat more to get the extra calories needed to gain weight and add to the layers of blubber under their skin that insulates them from the cold.

In all likelihood PJ would be transferred to another zoo in the spring before breeding season started. Our next challenge was to train him to voluntarily go into a crate for the transfer to his new home. The crate arrived. I did not want to think about not seeing him again, let alone not playing with him anymore. He was smart, fun, and brought joy to me every moment I was with him. In the ocean, he would have left his mother when he was about one year old. He was two and a half now. Nature said it was time to go and I understood. Still, I would miss him very much.

The crate training turned out not to be much of a challenge. PJ trusted his people. He was accustomed to entering and exiting a stainless-steel squeeze cage daily since he was a small pup. Our zoo purchased this cage in the 1990s to examine the sea lions when they were very ill. At the time, it was a state-of-the-art way to examine a sea lion. Now our animals allow us to touch them and examine them without restraint. PJ even chose to sleep in the squeeze cage with his mother, Star, when he could have selected to sleep anywhere is his indoor or outdoor habitat. It made me laugh when I came to work in the morning to see them spooning in this stainless-steel exam cage. They did not find it intimidating at all. It seems they found it cozy.

A new home was found for PJ. Before he left, he would be tranquilized for a medical exam. Exams like this are done routinely before a transfer to another zoo. I had worked on injection training PJ for about a year. He had never needed an injection before, but we practiced often so as to be prepared, touching him with a syringe without a needle, followed by a fish, of course. It desensitized him to the process and allowed me to build a strong trusting relationship with him. After a few times, he began to like the syringe touching him because he got a lot of praise and fish for participating in what he considered a game. In my experience, if you are teaching an animal, they learn faster when they are having fun. Repetition and reinforcement is the key to successful training. I could poke him with the syringe anywhere on his body. Repeating the process and reinforcing his calm acceptance of it with many fish had him looking forward to this routine. PJ was injected with ease and his physical determined that he was a healthy young sea lion.

His transfer day arrived, May 4, 2016. He hopped right into the crate ready for the ride to his new zoo home. We dropped the door of the crate and loaded him onto a truck with no complaints. The truck was air conditioned and we also had ice to keep his body temperature at a healthy level. I didn't accompany him, but two of my colleagues did. We were notified he arrived safely at the new facility. I was grateful he was safe, but a big piece of my heart went with him. PJ was a gift given to us after Puff's death. PJ, Star, and Angel helped me heal after Puff and Flounder passed. I am grateful for the time I had with them. Over the course of my career, I have been fortunate that very few animals in my care have been shipped to other facilities. Whether it is recognized or not, it is a loss when you care for and love an animal every day and cannot be with them again. I am sure Star and Angel missed him too. He was action wrapped up in a sea lion body, with never a boring moment.

Chapter 9
Every Birth Is a Miracle

Sunny and the snowman

Star, Angel, and Hut were putting on weight in preparation for the breeding/birthing season. Often sea lions do not eat during this time of year. Males pack on the pounds to become larger so they can spend their energy securing the best beaches and the most females. Females are busy either giving birth or being courted or bred by the males. Copulation can happen either on land or in water, but birth happens on land. All three of our sea lions gained about 30 pounds each between March and June. Hut certainly wasn't pregnant. What about our slightly rounded Star and Angel? Both females were trained to allow us to ultrasound them. A date was set to ultrasound both Star and Angel. However, the procedure was soon canceled because our vet staff found it necessary to schedule a complete physical on Hut due to concern about his health after the EEE. Also, an ophthalmologist would come to look at his eyes and they wanted further blood work done to get more information on EEE.

Veterinarians from other zoos were scheduled to visit our zoo to assist during the physical in hopes of learning more about this disease. Hut would have to be tranquilized for this thorough physical. Our job was to get his training for injections back up to speed. He could not eat before he was tranquilized for the same reason people cannot eat. We did not want him to aspirate food— that could be fatal. Hut's physical was set for June 20, 2016.

Well, Starfish had a different idea. The afternoon prior to Hut's physical, she was looking uncomfortable; she was holding her stomach and keeping her rear flippers squeezed together. Star separated herself from the others secluding herself in the inside holding room. I told my supervisor that Star might have other things planned for us tomorrow and we might not be examining Hut. Late that night Star gave birth to a very healthy female pup. We named the pup Sunfish, Sunny for short. A sun born from a star. This beautiful pup was born on Father's Day. Star was always full of surprises. Good girl! I was confident in her mothering abilities because Star had demonstrated that she was an excellent mother with PJ so I was not concerned about how Star would care for this pup and quite thrilled about the new adventures we would have.

The video camera we had installed to capture events in the inside sea lion holding area caught a glimpse of the pup's birth. Behind a pillar in the sea lion holding room in the wee hours of the morning one chubby sea lion became two. We smiled as we tried to make out the dark and fuzzy video. Every birth is a miracle!

We kept Star and the pup separate from the other sea lions for a while so they could bond without interruption. Star soon began vocalizing to the pup and the pup responded. Star was a "chatty Cathy," talking away and the pup would just look at her as if to say, "I was just born and that is a lot of information to understand." I just smiled and said to myself, "Star's got this." She could handle the challenges she was about to face; I was certain. I watched as she nudged the pup to a nipple. Star was so confident and happy. Having known her for most of her life, I could tell that Star was ecstatic. Together they were nudging, barking, and nursing. That holding room was noisy. The pup was awkward moving on land, tripping over its flippers on occasion. Star did not interfere often. She let the pup get up on her own and to learn on her own.

Almost immediately after birth, Star was already teaching the pup to follow her. We zookeepers laughed listening to Star vocalize louder and faster when the pup would turn and scoot the other way. We joked that the pup must be a female because it was not listening to her mother. Sure enough, I got close enough to the pup and confirmed it was a female!

This pup would often try to swim in the inside holding pool. Star was not ready for her little one to go in the water and would toss her up on dry land. Over and over Star would get her out of the water and calmly bark, "Don't do it again." Then as soon as Star's back was turned, splash, the pup had hopped into the pool again. Already headstrong (very similar to her mother), the pup began vocalizing as much as Star. They had full conversations about what one expected of the other. It was a delight listening to them.

The pup was a week old when Star trained her newborn to follow her to our scale to be weighed. Imagine the communication going on. I would call Star and she would call Sunny. You should have seen this process. I videotaped it so I could look back and marvel at the two of them. Sunny would be very close to the scale, then make a break for it and go to another room. You should have seen Star's face. "What the....?"And she was off rounding up the little imp. I could not help laughing out loud. "Yes," I thought to myself, "Star, I understand." I have two children of my own who did just what they wanted to and yes, it is worth it and yes, it is endless and exhausting, but what fun!

The pup weighed 22 pounds at one-week old. They lit up our lives with joy. Sunny soon took to the water like a mermaid.

We decided to let Star and Sunny outside with Angel and Hut sooner than our initial plan because Angel was looking a little uncomfortable and she was keeping to herself. Yes, a pup was on the way! We could not keep up with all the changes. June is a very busy time of year for the California sea lion whether in the ocean or here at our zoo. We knew these births would trigger Hut's hormones because breeding season naturally occurs one to three weeks after the pups are born.

Star took over the inside holding room as her pup sanctuary with Sunny. She made it apparent that no one was allowed in or out unless you were her trainer bringing food (often that was me and I was very cautious approaching them). That pup was number one in Star's life, as she should have been. Star was hormonally edgy and I was *very* respectful of my distance in relation to the pup. I did not want to risk our friendship at any cost. In the beginning, I didn't even acknowledge the pup. I just did a visual exam on both and got out of there.

Well, Angel decided she wanted to give birth in Star's pup sanctuary, the inside holding area. Star was guarding the entrance as Angel attempted to go in. Angel must have been very certain this was what she needed because only the brave, foolish, or desperate would consider trying to get by Star. In Angel's situation, she was probably all three. She became a powerhouse, barreled pass Star and the sleeping Sunny, and then slid into the entrance of the next room, the ISO room. Star was hot on her heels, mouth opened and vocalizing profusely. I did not want to intervene unless Angel really needed me. I watched with my hand on the door handle. If I felt they could not work this out themselves, I would enter the room and separate them. Their friendship was solid, but more than that, I trusted their instincts would resolve this. After all, female sea lions have given birth next to each other on the California coast every year for thousands of years. This was just Star and Angel's first time.

Star pushed Angel with her neck and Angel retreated to where I could not see them around a corner. Then Angel came back into sight; I saw that her mouth was open and she was pushing back with determination. Sunny awoke from her nap during this disruption and cried out softly. Star was at Sunny's side in an instant, glaring at Angel preparing to move Angel out of there, when Angel had another contraction and began pushing. Right in front of Star and me, Angel began to give birth. I held my breath and looked at Star who began watching as well.

Angel looked at her tail, adjusted her flippers and tensed up her body. Angel was five feet in front of the window where I stood viewing all this. Star and Sunny were approximately sixteen feet away. Sunny was rolling on her back with her little flippers raised in the air and moving slightly with Star right by her side watching Angel thoughtfully. I thought to myself, "Sunny gets a friend to play with!" Angel had wanted to be a mother since the birth of PJ. I was chirping inside. I pulled out my phone to record the birth. Other staff quietly peeked through the window and watched a miracle take place. Angel would be a first-time mom. We were so excited and happy for her. I never looked through the lens of my camera phone, I just held up it in a position to capture the event. I did not want to miss a thing.

Every Day Is a Gift

For four minutes and twenty-eight seconds she pushed, then readjusted her body and then pushed again. We all held our breaths and watched with Star. Angel gave a final big push, and the pup slid out. I realized that I was unconsciously pushing too. I stopped and took a breath. I could only see her face because during the delivery her bottom end went out of view behind a door. I was ready to hear her and that pup make the distinctive call mothers and pups make to each other at birth. I had not heard Angel vocalize since she was a pup herself. I could not wait to see the adventures they would have learning from one another.

I saw Angel clear the pup's mouth and she ate its contents. Silence. I looked at Star. She had lain down and continued to watch intently. Angel rolled the pup with her flippers, then picked it up with her mouth and dropped it. She knew just what to do to get that little one up and going. That would be exactly what we, her zookeepers, would do if she wasn't doing it herself. How did she know how to do this? It was amazing.

However, I was becoming concerned because the pup still hadn't made a sound. The second time Angel lifted the pup again to resuscitate it, the pup remained limp. I looked at my coworkers and I said, "I am going in." I stepped through the doorway to help Angel. I got on my knees so I was level with her. I told her she was a good girl and her baby was beautiful. I could tell the pup was dead. Angel looked directly into my eyes (her eyes are beautiful chocolate pools) and I could see her question, "What is going on?" She then turned to look at Sunny, who was still playing quietly on her back. Angel looked back at her pup and tried again to wake her baby up. Then she looked back into my eyes. I will take this memory to my grave. This event had to be the most pitiful thing I had ever seen in my thirty-plus years zoo career and trust me I have seen more than I care to mention.

The pup was not waking up, but Angel did not give up. She continued to move it around while taking quick peeks at Sunny.

We decided to remove Angel's pup from the holding room. It would be better for Angel not to bond with the pup. The vet staff needed to see what had caused Angel's pup's death. I examined the pup; it was a female. I laid my hand on its soft yet cold chest; she was so beautiful, perfectly formed and her coat was silvery grey. As I touched her chest, I said a quick prayer for all of us. I thought of the opportunity Angel had missed becoming a mother. "Dear Lord, please...." I knew He understood what we needed and what I meant even if I didn't at the time.

Angel didn't seem to mind us taking the pup. I think her mind hadn't grasped the events. Mine hadn't yet either. This entire ordeal from Angel's entrance to the holding room to the birth and death of her pup was approximately twenty minutes. Angel was our main concern now. She wasn't out of the woods yet as she still had to pass the afterbirth. We wanted to keep her inside so she could quietly expel the placenta.

Once again, she had other things on her mind. She took another look at Sunny and approached the pup. Star got in between them, but Angel blinded by hormones and grief ignored the facts and decided that Sunny was her pup. A fight began as Star moved to protect Sunny and Angel tried to take her as her own. They had never fought before. For about thirty seconds, I watched these best friends fight to be the mother of the only living pup until I saw Star conceding. I walked into the fight with a thick 4' x 6' plastic board in my hand. They both weighed a lot more than I do and their adrenaline was raging. I had to separate them. If I fell and got bit, that would not help the situation, so in one motion, with my adrenaline soaring as well, I put the board in between the pup and Angel. Both Star and Angel bit the board I was holding at the same time. "Well that didn't work," I said to myself.

Quickly I decided to open the outside door. Star made a motion to leave. Speaking in a tone of voice the sea lions had never heard me use, I said, "Not you, Star! Angel, outside!" I bumped the board on the ground twice and said, "Let's go, Angel, outside!" It was not a request. I had never raised my voice or used something to scare them. Sunny needed Star and Angel needed some space to let her placenta pass and to calm down. Within a couple of seconds Angel turned to go outside and I told her she was a good girl. After Angel left the holding area, I closed the outside door. Sunny and Star sniffed each other's noses and began to settle down.

I watched Angel for a couple of hours as she swam and swam to see if she would pass the placenta. At times, she would sit in front of the closed holding room door, calling inside for her pup. Seeing and hearing Angel call to her pup broke my heart again. This was the first time I heard her use her voice since she was eighteen months old.

I have read about broken heart syndrome. Animals including people have died from being too sad; hearts are damaged during stressful times and death can occurred. When Puff died in 2012, my chest hurt so much where my heart is and I cried so hard I thought I would die. I was hoping Angel was not feeling that way. I would never wish that heartache on anyone. Angel's health was our first concern. She had to get through this. I wished I could get a pup for her. There had to be an orphaned California sea lion pup somewhere in the nation that needed a doting mother. Too bad life doesn't work that way. I would have spent every penny I had to ship a pup to our zoo for Angel. But all I could do was watch her, wait with her, and pray.

We did not see the placenta pass, so she was given an injection to help the process. Yes, after all this, Angel allowed a hand injection. Unbelievable—the massive power of animal/human relationships and positive reinforcement training. We never found Angel's placenta. After the pup's birth, I was told by another facility that they had observed sea lion mothers eating their placentas.

The vet staff examined Angel's pup and found it was a stillbirth. It never took a breath. The pup was full term and looked healthy inside and out. I found out later that stillbirths are not uncommon among sea lions especially with first-time mothers.

We decided to keep Star and Sunny separated from Angel for a couple of weeks. Star and Sunny needed to continue bonding. Breeding season was due to begin again (remember, female sea lions become receptive to breeding a few weeks after they give birth). The birth of Angel's pup would trigger Hut's hormones and he would soon be interested in breeding Angel. We just had to wait and watch for Angel to become receptive to breeding.

A couple weeks after Angel's stillbirth, Hut's behavior began to change; he was barking and following Angel around, a clear indication that the breeding season was underway. He was courting both females. Hut only had to wait for them to be receptive. In the early afternoon on July 20, 2016, Hut and Angel were mating on the embankment in front of the doors where the keepers and sea lions enter and exit the habitat. Zoo staff and guests could observe their copulation. When Angel thought the duration was adequate, she turned around and put her mouth around Hut's right eye until he released her. Spunky little Angel sure knew how to get her message across!

On July 27 when Star became receptive, breeding occurred in the water on the west side of the sea lion habitat. I glanced over to the far side of the beach where Sunny was sleeping and then back again to Star and Hut, dreaming of the new pup and friend I may have next year. I watched Angel swim over for a moment for a closer look at Star and Hut breeding and smiled at the question in her eyes. We were all feeling hope once again.

A summer camp group was watching the breeding in progress. One child was concerned. She asked if the sea lions were hurting one another. I assured her they were not, that what she was observing was natural behavior. I pointed to the sleeping pup and said that was how Sunny came to be. The child looked at Sunny and then at me and smiled. Yes! I have the career dreams are made of. Helping people understand and love nature is only a part of the big picture. When you wake up in the morning, you never know what you will be observing or discussing when you are a zookeeper.

At one month old, Sunny, with a mind of her own, would follow Hut inside. Star would be the caboose of this pinniped train, frantically calling Sunny to her. We would laugh at Star's dismay and at Sunny's independence and then the look on Hut's face. The expression on his face seemed to say, "I did not sign up for this." Sunny was completely smitten with Hut. We would find her sleeping on his flipper or she would come uninvited to one of his training sessions and then just rest on him. We always told Hut what a good boy he was. Male sea lions usually do not nurture pups. Hut was the exception. We loved him even more.

Chapter 10
Star and the Sun

Star and Sunny on the high rock

Star's agenda for bringing up Sunny was close to the one she had for PJ—teaching her the ropes about how things were done. Star was more relaxed with this pup and I was happy to see her confident and at ease. In succession she taught Sunny to follow her inside, to go on the weight board, to swim in the inside pool, and then how to get out of that pool by herself. When these tasks were accomplished, Star shifted her focus to the outside beach. She began with teaching Sunny to follow her onto the beach and then, once in the water, how to avoid the filter system intakes and outputs. Once each life skill was completed to her satisfaction, she moved on to the next lesson. I watched with pride as my Starfish taught Sunny how to get out of the large pool in different places. With a camera in my hand to keep the memories, I made videos of Sunny and Star's accomplishments as I did and still do with my own children. She would call Sunny to a certain area of the beach.

If Sunny didn't respond to Star, Star would grab her by the scruff, take her to the area she had in mind, and then push her small pup with her nose to assist her up on land. I watched their interactions with wonderment and more than a little pride. That's my little Starfish being the best mother in town!

Once the easy skills were achieved, things grew more complex. Star decided Sunny was going to attend her mother's training sessions. I would call Star to me and we would begin her daily exam. I checked her eyes, touched her entire body to assess her overall physical health, and examined under her tail. Usually Star was silent during her training sessions. Since Sunny's birth, however, Star was fixated on having Sunny learn something during these training sessions. Star would bark and honk for Sunny until Sunny joined us. Star had acted this way with PJ too and I thought it was fantastic. The only differences I noticed between the two pups was that Star would reward PJ with her milk for his cooperation and that PJ was a month older than Sunny when Star decided it was time for her pups to begin learning from her humans. Star would call and call and Sunny would come, but with obvious hesitation, keeping to the side of Star that was farthest from me.

Please remember Sunny was about four weeks old and this mother and daughter were communicating clear enough for humans to understand. This was truly remarkable. Star honked and barked until her very young pup would switch sides and she was nearly on my lap. I was petting Star at the time. It appeared Star wanted Sunny to be part of this tactile session. What else could it mean? This would happen time and time again. I did not want to foul this up by petting the pup. Cleary, Sunny did not want to be touched; her body language spoke volumes. Star and I had done this routine for years. Star knew exactly what to do during these sessions and she knew what I would do. We trusted each other, but Sunny hadn't reached that point with me yet.

Next, I asked Star to go up on the highest rock on the beach. She swam over to the land and hopped up the rock work and beckoned Sunny, telling her, "Follow me here, climb up here." And there Sunny would follow, all 35 pounds of her, obeying orders. Up the rock she went to be with Star. Star knew what came next—the big dive—then back up on land in front of me. I signaled with my hand for Star to begin. Star looked at her little sidekick, gave her a honk, and dove in. I was cracking up. That poor kid, she was in the womb a month ago and now her mom had her diving off a high rock. Star was back by my side in seconds and she turned to look behind her as we watched Sunny unceremoniously plunk in the water. Star gave a honk and Sunny was soon hopping out of the water and sitting with us not looking as pleased as Star was. I was with a new sea lion trainer on the beach at that time. She did not realize that Star was giving Sunny lessons. I asked Star to do it again and the entire mother-teaching-daughter process was repeated. The new sea lion trainer opened her mouth in awe. It dawned on her what she was seeing and she was speechless. Again, I can only say, "Star was amazing!"

On September 14, 2016, we decided to bring in the ultrasound machine into the sea lion holding and get Star used to being touched by its wand again. She and Hut had bred almost two months previously. By February, we would be able to see the fetus on an ultrasound, with an expected birth in June or July. It had been three years, when Star was pregnant with PJ, since we last practiced using this machine with Star. We would ask Star to hold still near the sonography machine while we rubbed her stomach with a wand. Star and I practiced the routine during two of our training sessions that day. Star was very patient and trusting with me and this machine. Since Star concentrated better during training when she and Sunny were not in the same room (Star would most likely invite Sunny to observe the training), we kept Sunny outside. After our final training session of the day, I told her she did a great job and gave her a big hug and lots of fish. I told her, "We'll go outside now and see Sunny."

As soon as we left the holding area to go outside, Star began vocalizing for Sunny. I realized it was Sunny's turn now that Star and I had finished her lesson. Star was such a hoot. I was petting Star telling her to have a good weekend because I was off the next couple of days and here came Sunny, while Star was still barking, giving Sunny directions on her next task. My arm was around Star (I loved holding her) who continued talking to Sunny when Sunny stopped in front of me and rested her head on my knee. Star became quiet. Sunny was touching me, not me touching her, and then she looked up at me with her tiny peanut face. She was timid but her eyes sparkled in the light on that sunny afternoon. Star was under my left arm looking quite pleased because her daughter did as she requested. I gave Star a little squeeze and I said, "Thank you, Starfish. You are a very good girl." I gave her the rest of her fish dinner and she and Sunny hopped away together and jumped in the pool for a swim. This is a moment I will forever cherish.

The next day was the beginning of my weekend. I was cleaning my house and thinking of Star throughout the day and looking forward to the next lesson she would teach Sunny when my home phone rang. It was a work colleague and she asked me if I was sitting down. I thought of all the animals I help care for and told her I was getting seated. She said Star was dead. According to a visitor who witnessed it, Star threw her head back and fell into the outside pool and stopped moving. Our staff was there in minutes and pulled Star out of the water, but she was already dead.

I grabbed my chest and I wondered if my heart could possibly take any more sadness. I became dizzy and my vision blurred. I wished I had passed out, because I did not want to process what I was just told. I asked my colleague to please stay on the phone with me. I did not want to be alone. We cried together. At that moment, my husband came home from work three hours early. He never comes home from work early. I guess God did not want me to be alone either because I had sunk into a very dark place. I had lost Star. Grasping that I would never see her or touch her or play with her again was filling me with so much loss and pain, I could not breathe, so I began to pray. I prayed for strength and peace. Through God's mercy I received it. I was strong enough to call a dear friend and tell her of our loss and then I drove to pick her up so we could go comfort and be comforted by my coworkers.

While I was driving to pick up my friend the phone in my car rang. I pulled into a parking lot. It was another good friend of mine who also works at the zoo. She asked me what I was doing and I said, "Crying and driving." She said, "So you heard about Star." I said I had and I was on my way to the zoo. I told her about the day before—my last day with Star and how much I loved her. I was able to express to her what I was feeling.

I understand every day is a gift. I absolutely treat every day as one. I loved Star with my entire heart and Star knew it. Every day I made sure she did. All the animals I care for, know I love them and so do my human friends and family. I only wish we had more time together.

Because of what the witnesses saw, I was told, the vet staff believed Star's death came from a seizure, but her necropsy hadn't occurred yet so they were not certain. What we did know at the time was that Sunny was an orphan now. At Star's death, a docent saw Sunny underwater trying to wake Star up. She said it was one of the most heart-rending scenes she had ever watched.

Chapter 11
Path and Direction

Angel and Sunny playing at the gallery glass

After Star's death, I would wake up at night with flashes of light, my heart pounding and tears smeared on my face while crying out, "I can't do this anymore." I prayed for peace. I asked God to show me what He wanted me to do. He answered my prayers when I met Madeline. I was in the grocery store parking lot with a bag of groceries in my arms. I set the bag on the truck and was fumbling for my keys and I looked up to see this petite woman smiling at me. She may have been twenty years older than I and at least six inches shorter. She asked me if I needed help with my bag. I smiled at her and thought, "Boy I must look a wreck if she is offering me help." I said, "No, thank you."

We began talking. We discussed our children and the challenges of life. Then our conversation turned to God. We shared the blessings in our life and how much we trust and love Him. She shared that she was adopted when she was a child. What a coincidence! I was adopted as well. Late in life she adopted six children. There are many challenges to being a parent. It is hard for me to imagine parenting six young children when you are over forty years old. This woman accepted those challenges in God's name. She became stronger than she ever could have imagined. Like her also, my husband and I adopted our children. After loving our children for so long and being loved by them I do forget sometimes that I didn't actually carry them inside me and give birth to them and that my mother didn't actually conceive me.

The message I got out of our meeting is that we are all God's children. I believe we begin in heaven and through our life become closer or farther away from God. It is our choice. It is always our choice. We talked for almost an hour. Madeline then hugged me and said she loved me and I said I loved her back. Two strangers who now loved each other—that is God at work. As I was driving to my son's soccer game, I felt less pain than I did before I met Madeline. I truly believe Madeline was a messenger from God. On the way to the store that evening, my heart was hurting and I was praying for peace. The pain of losing Star was almost too much for me to handle and then there came Madeline. I felt loved and not alone. God is good. Maddie did not know sea lions, but she knew love and loss. We all do. We all have pain and challenges. We all struggle. How you handle it and how we evolve and grow as children of God is what counts. Should I move on from my zoo job? Was thirty years working at the zoo enough? Did God want me to praise Him in another way? I prayed and prayed.

Then, as always, the animals reopened my eyes to the beauty of living in the moment. The grey wolves, the newest members of the zoo family, would hop up on each other and then play bow to me obviously happy to see me. They were afraid of the other keepers and our zoo guests. For six months, they had been our hyena's neighbors. Every day I would call Lou, the spotted hyena, to me, telling him he was a "good boy," and give him a raw meat treat for coming to me. He would spin around and play games that he created with me. I was so lucky to be part of his merriment. I would laugh and watch the fuzzy hair on the very top of his head as it blew in the wind. He would have a gleam of excitement in his eyes because he chose me to be his friend. Day after day, when I got up to leave Lou, I would see the wolves quietly observing my encounter with him. In the earlier days, they would run away when they saw me look at them. I never engaged them in any way because I was not taking care of them at the time and I knew they feared people. I believe watching my interactions with Lou is the reason the wolves chose me to be their friend. Now when I passed their habitat, they made whining noises and bounced up and down when they saw me. I certainly did not appear dangerous to them as they watched me talking sweetly to the hyena every morning and evening.

On March 12, 2019 (my birthday) the female wolf, Willow, allowed me to touch her for the first time. I used a pen to touch her shoulder. Her only reaction was to hold perfectly still. This birthday gift I will never forget. To gain trust from an innocent, fragile animal I cannot describe. I felt that now I owed her everything I could possibly give to make her life full of fun and free of fear. She allowed me to hand inject her for the first time on April 30, 2019. She trotted over, in her sweet apprehensive way. Her brother was there eating. She entered the "chute" I made out of a flipped over water trough. I gave her the shot; she jumped away because the medicine does sting. Then I walked away quickly. I was very worried she would never trust me again or her brother Timber would be traumatized seeing his sister being taken away by zookeepers to the animal hospital. Willow received a clean bill of health after her exam. The best part of this story was at the end of this day, when Willow fully recovered from the anesthesia; both wolves came to me when I called! I gave them delicious meat treats and thanked God they decided we were going to have a future together full of patience and understanding.

The Amur tigers and I had a morning routine; they would crouch down and hide, pupils big with anticipation as I walked by, waiting for me to hide and pop out in the same manner. I had taught them to go on a weight board, receive injections voluntarily, and now we were working on drawing blood from their tails. We enjoyed our training time together.

With every interaction with the animals, my pain lessened.

Chapter 12
Hope and Loss

Only three months old and still nursing, Sunny depended on her mother greatly. Star had taught her many lessons, but Sunny still had so much to learn. We immediately started offering Sunny bottles of gruel, ice-cubed fish, fish pieces, and live fish. We locked Angel inside with Sunny, hoping Angel would begin lactating. The first few days were not too bad for Sunny. She was a chunky little milk-fed pup and she was seen drinking water out of the hose. Sea lions do not drink water in the wild because the ocean is salt water. They stay hydrated from the fish they eat and pups stay hydrated from mother's milk. We knew Sunny was hydrated because she was playing and looking vibrant. She would vocalize every so often by the outside door which was closed, but her mom could no longer answer. When Sunny did vocalize, we knew she was hungry and if we were in the area to hear her call we would bring her fish or offer a bottle. For obvious reasons, she didn't know what a bottle was. I remember watching one of my colleagues crawl to Sunny on his hands and knees offering her a bottle. She thought he was nuts and so did I. Sunny hopped away and I stood there smiling. The effort and good intentions were there and it gave me hope. I knew that I certainly was not alone in this. Sunny was loved and we were going to get her through this.

109

We started by offering her live fish. Sunny began catching them. Two days later she began catching and then eating them. Next, she began eating the cut-up dead fish we put in small ice cubes, but it was not enough to fill her up. She needed to eat pounds of the nutritious herring and capelin to get the calories that would equal her mother's milk. She began vocalizing more and looking to Hut and Angel for food. Neither of them was lactating, so I began entering the sea lion area frequently and tossing fish into the pool. Sunny knew her name and would come running or in this case hopping over. I would throw live fish, dead fish, and ice-cube fish into the pool. One day she ate one hundred live minnows and we had to rush out to our supplier to buy more.

I awoke thoughtful on October 4, 2016, the feast of Saint Francis, the patron saint of animals and the fourth anniversary of Puff's death. He has been in my heart since the day I met him. Death could not change that. In my morning prayer, I imagined him and Star playing with the door stop they enjoyed and were not supposed to have. They were playing keep-away like they did years ago and in my mind I saw God smiling at them, his little creations, shaking His head at their mischief. I believe we are with our loved ones in heaven when we die. This belief keeps me going. I prayed that morning for tiny Sunny, Angel, and Hut along with all the people and animals I love.

When I got to work, Sunny was calling for food. I immediately entered the sea lion holding area and offered her both live and dead fish. She gobbled up the live fish but left the capelin as usual. When she began to call again, I gave her the rest of the live fish. A total of three pounds! I tossed her cut up herring and some whole capelin. We were running out of the live fish for the day so the next time she called I gave her only dead fish so there would be live fish for her dinner. At 11:30 a.m. precisely, the same time Puff died four years ago, Sunny ate her first dead fish! She ate the same nutritious fish our adult sea lions eat, but she ate like a penguin, gulp, gulp, swallow. God is good.

Sunny had been vocalizing her hunger for over a week. At last she was silent because she was eating and her stomach was finally full! My coworkers and I had entered the area to feed Angel and Hut when I saw Sunny gulp down her first fish. We, her people, quietly hugged each other and smiled, watching her for minutes. We did not cheer out loud for fear she would become afraid and discontinue eating. Every time she ate a capelin, I would toss another fish near her in the pool and she would eat it. We counted fourteen fish. That was an entire pound of capelin. I stopped at that amount as I did not want her to get ill; her stomach may not have been ready for more. We were thrilled.

Sunny ate four pounds of fish that day and went on eating like a little champ. She became strong and healthy just like her mom. Sunny played every day with a variety of enrichment items. She liked the water stream from the hose. It must have felt good in her tiny mouth. I would leave the hose running on the beach and she would engage with its spray for hours. Pine cones, ice, sticks, leaves, and visits from our pool maintenance staff with their long poles and leaf nets kept her busy all day.

In autumn, I bought a gourd at the public market. I watched as she practiced porpoising over this bumpy pumpkin all afternoon as her human friends watched and smiled at her capers. She began asking Angel to play with her by bringing a stick over to Angel or bobbing her head in an inviting way. Slowly Angel was beginning to warm up to Sunny and for this I was grateful. Since Star's death Angel largely ignored Sunny and discontinued playing with the enrichment items she used to enjoy. Angel and Star were friends for years. It appeared Angel was mourning the death of her dear friend. Sunny enjoyed seeing her reflection in a mirror propped on the other side of the gallery glass and engaged the pup in the mirror with toys or spinning antics. Like all children, she was learning through play. In a few weeks she went up to forty-two pounds and was gaining weight daily. Even after the death of her mother, Sunny continued to go on our sea lion weight scale when we asked. We were very fortunate Sunny had had such a bright enthusiastic teacher. Because of Star we were still able to monitor her pup's growth.

We picked up her training where her mother left off. We used the kind and gentle approach that we have always used, positive reinforcement. At four months old, she came when she was called, went into the inside holding area from outside, dunked her eyes in a tub of salt water for general eye health, and allowed us to touch her to begin the injection training process.

Hut had been acting quieter than usual and not eating as much. Sunny found comfort in lying on him when they slept. We weren't sure if he was depressed from Star's death or it was a health issue. I know Hut and Star liked each other because I found them sleeping together often. When Sunny began eating more she became independent of Hut and Angel, sleeping by herself. Watching her mature at such a young age and sleep alone brought tears to my eyes, but that is what a survivor, a fighter, does. They become independent and she was a survivor. Sunny played with the toys we gave her and like PJ enjoyed playing at the underwater viewing glass with her friends on the other side—the keepers, docents, volunteers, other staff, and visitors.

Chapter 13
Hut

On October 21, 2016, I was on an out-of-state trip. While in the middle of the Arizona desert, I received a phone message that must have been floating in the cloud for a while. It was from a coworker asking me to call her as soon as I could. I thought of all the animals I cared for. I was very concerned. I would be called while away on a trip only if it were an emergency. The voice calling part of my phone would not work but the texting part did. I wrote that I didn't know when service would connect and that I was very concerned about her call. "Please let me know what is going on." She wrote back, "At 3:55 p.m. today Hut passed away." She explained that he had refused food and was swimming inside when the surveillance camera caught him acting irregularly. Two of my coworkers saw he was struggling. They ran into the holding room to see if they could help. They called the vet staff, but Hut was dead in seconds. They attempted to resuscitate him; unfortunately, he did not wake up. A thorough exam would be performed to see what the cause of death was. Months later blood tests concluded Hut passed away from congestive heart failure due to the mosquito-borne illness EEE that he'd contracted the previous summer.

I began crying when I heard the news. Once again God was good. I was not alone at the time. I was with my husband and another Christian couple we had recently met. I told the wife I was ready to leave my job. God obviously wanted me somewhere else. She said she believed I was wrong, that my love for these animals was a gift from God and a service to God. She listened carefully to my story as I cried. She also believed that Star left me a gift to love, Sunny, and that I could not deny Sunny the same love I gave her mother. She said Star was so wonderful because of the unconditional love that her humans gave her. This lady hardly knew me. When I first met her, she told me she never liked zoos because she thought the animals were treated poorly. Her opinion has changed since our conversation. I knew through the pain and the tears she was right, that I could not give up on them now when they needed me the most. God gave me this new friend to deliver this message right at the moment I needed help with the pain.

When we got back to our hotel room the flood works opened. My husband, concerned for my health, said I should try to stop crying; it was not healthy to cry so hard. I did not apologize. I knew what I needed to do to heal. I prayed for peace and peace came. I thought about how truly blessed I am to be able to love this much. Some people never allow themselves to be this vulnerable or to love as much as I have been fortunate enough to love.

Chapter 14
The Sweet Reunion

Sunny climbing on her mother, Star

On December 11, 2016, Sunny and Angel were locked in the sea lion inside holding area to allow for outside pool maintenance. Sunny had been seen playing with a piece of metal wire and the pool needed to be drained to see if there was more. The video camera that records the sea lions' actions inside the holding area recorded a playful Sunny. Soon Angel and Sunny were sleeping together for the night. The next day they would be given access to their outside habitat as soon as the aquatic life support staff had checked the water's quality.

The next morning, I came into the diet kitchen which connects to the inside sea lion holding room. I heard Sunny calling. I peeked in the room where she and Angel had spent the night. She saw me through the window in the door and called again while looking directly at me. This call was not the hunger call she used to tell us she was ready to eat. This one definitely said to me she was ready to go out for the day. I told her, "Okay, Sunny; one minute, Peanut." I radioed the aquatic life support staff and asked if they approved the pool for the sea lions' use. He responded "yes." I was happy I could do what Sunny wanted me to do when she asked. If I continued reinforcing our communications, Sunny would soon be communicating with me like Star did. We would connect with each other, trust each other, become friends. Star's little treasure that she left to us to love was strong, smart, and quite adorable. She did not have the handicaps her mother had when Star was born and growing up. Star was conceived, born, and shot in a polluted ocean, risked starvation, and had to contend with sharks and orcas. Sunny had a safe, fun environment with Angel, toys, and her people to give her a great life. Was she going to be more like her mom or dad? Probably her own little sea lion. The future was bright.

I entered the holding room and said, "Are you guys ready to go outside?" I slid the door open to allow Angel and Sunny access to their outside beach and pool. It had snowed the night before. Angel and Sunny bounded by me into the snow, up over the embankment, and splashed into the water. I left the area for a moment to find a shovel to clear the sea lion beach. It was a cold and quiet morning. My fellow zookeepers were shoveling the steps to the sea lion overlook and tossing it into the sea lion habitat as I was clearing the beach. We were talking to each other during our snowy morning routine, telling jokes, and commenting that Sunny

116

liked the snow being tossed in the pool. This wasn't her first snow and she seemed to like it. On previous snowy days, we would watch her appear quietly from playing underwater to where we tossed the snow. At times, I would build her a small snowman and she would remove the sticks I had placed in the snowman as arms or I would toss her snowballs like I did last winter in games I played with PJ. Today I just shoveled quickly because all the animals at the zoo needed their gates and pathways cleared from the recent snowfall. I quickly hosed the beach with warm water to clear any ice. Then I salted the beach for better traction for the sea lions, zookeepers, and the aquatic life support staff.

Usually during the morning cleaning, Sunny would come over to me asking with her liquid brown eyes to play the hose game. I would make the stream of water go in a circle and she would follow it, gently and playfully tracking it underwater. This morning she popped up once from the outside pool looking at me with the timid playful glint I was getting used to seeing, so I gave her a quick hose stream circle. She followed it for a moment then stopped. I was too caught up in the busy morning to initiate play with Sunny like I usually did. She didn't ask me again and I never thought too much about it because I had to prepare their diets and feed them that Monday morning. Our routine was to weigh them on Mondays before the first feeding. I had to set up the scales. I was guessing to myself how much the little peanut gained since last week while I was hustling away at my duties. I left the beach to get the scales to bring to the sea lion inside holding area and prepare their morning fish.

On my way to the sea lion area earlier that morning, I had hung Sunny's Christmas stocking, which I had designed the night before, in front of the gallery glass for zoo visitors to see. The golden glitter glue was dry now and read "Sunny' in cursive lettering. It was a smaller stocking than Angel's and it looked festive there, hanging for Christmas lovers to appreciate. The animals in my care were healthy and playful. I felt good! My coworkers and I were joking around with each other about various subjects. It was starting out to be a really good day. I went into the sea lion holding room with the scales laughing at my colleagues' jokes.

Since Sunny started eating fish, she responded to us flawlessly when we called her name to come inside. Because of positive reinforcement training, this tiny peanut, at five months old, would recognize her name when she heard it called, stop what she was doing (remember she is a wild animal without a mother), jump out of the water, and hop down the embankment through a large metal door (and allow us to close that door) every day at every feeding. We were calm and gentle with her. I treated her with the most professional gentleness, because we did not have a bond yet. With her mother, I could be exuberant, excited and boisterous. I treated Sunny like a fragile flower; I was calmer and more precise than I was with Angel when Angel arrived in 2011.

This was the beautiful beginning of a trusting bond between a human and a non-human animal. I have been very fortunate to be a part of such a bond many times before, but not like I was feeling with Sunny, the sweetest of innocents. Star's little gift was loved and cherished by her caregivers, the entire zoo staff, and the visitors, volunteers, and docents. I was going to enjoy every moment of her life. I did not want to rush my time with her. Her brilliant mind in that tiny body left me breathless. Watching her grow and understand words that we put to behaviors was amazing. Her little body, eyes filled with interest, and those bitty ears, the size of my thumb nail, captured my heart. A human child at 5 months old would not know how to respond like this sea lion pup. I was enjoying every second watching Sunny thrive. Sunny was Angel's new best friend and a new family member for me.

The scales were in place in the inside holding area and I opened the outside door to call Sunny inside. We trained the sea lions to come inside every day, entering the holding room in the same order at each feeding. Sunny always came in with Star and Star was always before Angel. The animals decided the order initially by hierarchy and we reinforced the calm entrance of each animal. Even after Star's passing, Angel allowed Sunny to come inside and eat first. Animals usually like a routine and it appeared Angel had not considered she should eat before Sunny.

I was very proud of the gentle choices Angel made, making her a good role model for Sunny. I stepped out on the sea lion beach and called "Sunny, let's go." Many times she would be waiting on the beach near the door. Today I had to give her another call, "Sunny, let's go." She may have been playing in the deep part of the pool and could not hear me. I walked up two steps and glanced over the edge where I saw Sunny, her mouth at the top of the water, not looking at me just floating. I called her again and she swam away quickly like she was afraid and I had startled her. "Strange," I thought to myself. Angel was waiting patiently through all this so I called her in for her turn to reinforce her patience. This was the first time I fed Angel before Sunny. Many animals I know would not wait so sweetly. Angel's patience and resilience are two of her many strengths.

Angel came inside, hopped on the scales and I weighed her. She weighed 202 pounds. Then I gave her the daily exam beginning with her eyes, skin and teeth, and proceeding through all the behaviors to which we asked her to respond. She passed with flying colors. I then let her outside and called Sunny again. Sunny did not jump up and greet me. She swam away startled again. I was beginning to be concerned. Maybe it was a new game she was playing, but my gut told me differently. She was seen playing with something earlier and maybe this novel toy had her attention. I was still concerned, trying to find reasons for her inexplicable behavior.

I left the area to feed and check on the other animals in my area. I decided I would come back to Sunny in a half hour to see if she was ready for her morning routine. I watched her from the underwater viewing gallery for a few moments. She appeared to be tired; floating underwater with her eyes closed like sea lions do when they are tired. Maybe she had a bad night's rest. Time would tell.

I walked to the hyena's habitat. I had just asked Lou to switch to his holding area for the day's cleaning when I heard on the radio that Sunny looked ill and appeared to need help immediately. I locked things up and ran the one hundred yards in the snow in my winter boots. I met two of my coworkers at the entrance to our diet kitchen that subsequently leads to the sea lion habitat. They were both rushing to aid Sunny. One of my colleagues told me Sunny was lying on the bottom of the pool very still. In one swoop, I called on the two-way radio for our vet staff to come to the sea lion area, grabbed a long skimmer pole off the wall, quickly ran through the sea lion holding area to the outside beach, directly following the other zookeepers to aid Sunny. I dropped the pole in the water where my coworkers were pointing, but could not reach Sunny who was not moving on the bottom of the 10-foot deep pool.

The air temperature was 28 degrees; the pool water was 47 degrees. I looked at my coworker and when our eyes met we knew what had to be done.

He said, "I am going in to get her."

I said, "Take off your boots first."

He pulled off his shoes and dove into the water. He was at the bottom of the pool in a second. He pushed Sunny up through the water so I could grab ahold of her and pull her out. I clutched her little flippers and raised her head out of the water. Another coworker was next to me and together we quickly pulled Sunny onto land. I opened her small mouth with my fingers and looked into her throat quickly for any obvious foreign body and then began clearing her mouth and throat with my fingers. There were no obstructions in her airway. In a futile attempt to revive her, I started chest compressions and water came out of her mouth. But it was no use; I knew she was dead because of the lifelessness in her eyes and the limpness of her body.

At that same moment I realized my coworker was trying to get out of the frigid pool. For a sea lion, the water was tepid, but for a human it was at a dangerous temperature. I rolled Sunny to my dry coworker and she continued resuscitation attempts while I helped my friend out of the brisk water. I didn't want to lose him too. We picked up Sunny and rushed her inside where the vet staff also tried to resuscitate her. They declared Sunny dead. We all stood gathered around Sunny.

This feeling was all too familiar. We held hands and held Sunny. I put my hand on her little chest and I prayed. Immediately I knew she was with Star. I imagined them greeting each other at heaven's gates. With all the bark-honking and sniffing, I am sure Sunny's entrance made heaven a noisy place. I am also sure Star had been calling Sunny since the day Star passed away. We all held each other and cried. We were devastated at the loss of Sunny; the sea lion staff suffered together.

Chapter 15
God's Mercy

Angel playing peek-a-boo

Angel was underwater during Sunny's death and our attempted rescue. I did not see her, but I sensed she was watching quietly. My heart broke for her. Even now as I write this my chest aches and I cry for her loss as well as my own. Of course, there was no way I could explain things to her. She just had to survive like she always had. I had to ignore my pain and "act happy" when I was with her. Angel needed her people now more than ever.

Angel came inside when I called her a few hours after Sunny's death. She looked confused. I put my arms around her and, crying softly, I told her we would get through this. For her sake, I contained my sobs. She ate her entire bucket of fish. After she finished, I saw her looking around for Sunny. I gave her extra toys to play with while I talked gently to her. What else could I do? Later I saw her search slowly around the inside area and then with more desperation throughout her outdoor habitat. I wanted to take this pain away from her with my entire being. All the knowledge or money in the world could not change what happened, but God can heal the pain if we allow Him in our hearts. My heart swelled up with a lump in my throat as I watched Angel and prayed for mercy.

I had the next day off from work. I told my supervisors if Angel needed anything to let me know and I would come into work. She would be on my mind and in my prayers every moment. That night and many nights after my dreams were of pulling Sunny from the water; then bolts of lightning flashed in my head to awaken me with a feeling of shaking, trembling, loss and despair. My doctor told me these are symptoms of Post-Traumatic Stress Disorder (PTSD). My body and mind weren't handling this third loss. I prayed for strength and mercy.

I did receive a phone call from work two days after Sunny's death. One of my supervisors called and left a message on my voicemail saying that Angel wasn't doing well and if I wanted to come in to see if I could help I could. I was grocery shopping at the time. I left the store immediately.

I drove by my parent's street on the way to the zoo and I thought to myself "Boy I have to use the bathroom." (I know, too much information). I remember my Father calling from his chair asking who was coming into the house as I was relieving myself. I entered his resting area and let him know it was me. I told him about Angel. I really looked at him and I saw a very sick Dad and I felt guilty sharing my worry with him, but I saw understanding in his eyes. He smiled at me weakly, his eyes full of love as he looked at me. Now I know what my children see when I look at them. Then he fell back to sleep.

I did not know what to expect when I saw Angel and I certainly did not want to lose her to broken heart syndrome. I tried not to imagine the worse scenario as I prayed hard for Angel's health and my sanity. "God please help us," I prayed as I drove. I remember entering the zoo parking lot in a mental fog and knowing I had almost a half-mile walk until I was in the Rocky Coasts gallery where I could see Angel and talk with the staff about her behavior. Since I had been grocery shopping, I did not have my work keys with me and all the staff was at a meeting when I arrived. I entered the Rocky Coasts gallery and saw Angel lying on the bottom of the pool, very still. My mind would not tolerate another loss. I took a deep breath and I became the zoo professional that I am and have trained to be. This is my job and this is what I have done for over thirty years. I know animal behavior and if I can help I know where to start and I needed to start by connecting with my friend, Angel.

I watched her lying at the bottom of the pool. Sometimes she would rest underwater like this, but her body posture and the location she was lying in were not usual. My heart shook again thinking about all the members of my sea lion family that I had loved so much that had died and the possibility of this zoo habitat being empty. I fell into a dark place of hopelessness.

I thought of all the losses Angel had endured. She survived in the ocean for about one year until she was shot. Then she overcame all the trials of possible disease, pollution of the ocean, and the rehabilitation at the marine mammal center in California. Angel became more resilient on her flight to New York from

California. She became great friends with Flounder, Puff, and Star only to see them all die; a year and a half after her arrival, she witnessed Puff's accident and death; six months later she was with Flounder as he lost his battle with kidney failure. Less than three years later PJ with whom she played every day left our zoo to live at a new zoo. Angel was in the sea lion habitat when Star had her seizure and died and she watched our desperate attempts at resuscitation. She witnessed Hut's EEE and congestive heart failure and death, and then Sunny's loneliness and cries of hunger after Star passed, which taxed us all. Then Sunny died. In addition, Angel endured the hormonal challenges of being bred for the first time, her pregnancy, and subsequently the loss of her stillborn pup.

I stared at Angel and my thoughts drifted into the abyss; you suffer too when someone you love suffers. Then she half opened one eye. I was the only person in the Rocky Coasts gallery; all was quiet and I raised my hand to her. I turned it on, the smile, the waving, the running back and forth, while tossing my gloves at the window. Angel watched. Yes! She opened both eyes as she lay there and I felt a surge of hope. I kept up my foolishness and ever so slowly she floated to the glass directly in front of me. I wanted to scream, "I am sorry" and cry until I slept. The look in her eyes was as hopeless as mine was a moment ago and I knew I needed to help her out of this because that is what friends do.

Remember, I did not have my work keys and the animal staff was at a meeting. When Angel returned to the bottom of the pool and shut her eyes, I knew I needed to get with her quickly. It is the same feeling you have when your children, spouse, or parents need you; a driven urgency. Then a member of the aquatic support team walked into the Rocky Coasts gallery. After I told him that I was without my keys, he unlocked the sea lion area for me.

I saw there were fish at the bottom of the pool. We never toss fish at an animal that is not hungry. It is not good for the water quality in the pool where they live. I understood our staff was desperate for a reaction from Angel. I brought a toy and a few fish in her food bucket and walked out on the sea lion beach, not sure what I would do, but knowing I would give my all.

I tapped the stainless-steel food bucket on the beach because I knew she could hear that underwater. I watched through the crystal clear pool water as she moved slightly. I tossed a fish in the water and I called her name. I was alone; there was not a zoo employee or guest to be seen on this crisp winter's afternoon. I tossed a toy in the pool and it made a small splash in the water. I watched as she floated up to it slowly with one eye open. She was close to the surface so I began talking to her playfully and excited like I do when I am teaching her something new. I tossed another fish, fast and far from her, she usually likes to chase fish when I throw them in this manner. I was desperate for her to show me she was healthy. She looked at me. I asked her to do her favorite behavior. A behavior she made up herself. She slowly went to the glass and touched it with her nose! I smiled, threw my arms up it the air and shouted, "YAY! GOOD GIRL!" Then she began swimming. She swam and swam looking at me from underwater at times, but not slowing her fast pace. I called her to me so I could pet her. She didn't come to me, but that was okay because she was moving. The next day she began eating. She had turned a corner and I felt she was going to get through this. We were going to do everything in our power to help her.

By the end of January, she was eating like a champ and gained 25 pounds! There was a very good chance she had become pregnant just a few months ago before Hut died. We had watched the copulation on land in July. The only time she weighed this much before was when she was pregnant. Her nipples became enlarged in February and she gained an additional seven pounds. She was calm and happy and at times played tag with me at the gallery glass. We gave her ice blocks with fish frozen in them to satisfy her need to solve puzzles.

We all need to work to obtain food. Hand feeding an animal continually takes away an extremely important part of their life, hunting if you are a predator, searching if you are a forager. It is essential to a healthy body and mind, for all of us. I "hunt" for bargains to fulfill my puzzle-solving needs. Angel would hold the ice-block in her flippers as if they were hands and carry it through the water waiting for the chunk to melt a little and she was able to pick the fish from the ice. She enjoyed the extra time we keepers spent with her and the assortment of toys we gave her throughout the day especially the motion-activated, singing animatronic fish she liked turning on. One day we set up five of these silly toys along the gallery glass. I watched as she approached each one on the other side of the glass and turned each one on individually in succession until they were all singing different songs and wiggling strangely in unison. I was happy she chose to restart them often after they finished their songs because I knew she was having a good time. I rubbed her stomach every day I was with her as I told her what a good girl she was. I took many pictures and videos of her growth and her overall positive attitude. I was very happy she was thriving and I was storing up memories against the future, treating every day as the gift it is.

Chapter 16
Dad

On April 3, 2017, I had just arrived at the Rocky Coasts diet kitchen to begin my duties for the day when I checked my phone and saw that both my mother and my husband had called me many times that morning as I traveled to work. I checked my voice mail and heard that my father fell again at home and was rushed to the hospital in an ambulance. I told my supervisor and coworkers about my dad and I left work, praying all the while for my dad and my mom.

I arrived at the hospital and was told my dad was in ICU. I went to the ICU waiting room, a room I was all too familiar with, a room I had spent hours waiting and praying for one of my parents at one time or another. My mother, brothers, and husband met me there and Mom told me the story of that morning and the previous evening. She said the night before my dad was talking through the night and was not making sense. Dad suffered from congestive heart failure and that morning he had an appointment to see his cardiologist. Dad had had a major heart attack twelve years prior to this hospitalization. They called that heart attack "the widow maker." He lived through that major heart attack and had one heart valve that worked (donated by a pig). For a long time, he had been living on less than twenty percent heart function. Mom told me that Dad did not want to go to the hospital again; he wanted to be at home. Years ago, he told my family with a smile, that we would have to carry him out of his house because his blood and sweat built that home. Mom said that morning Dad was very uncomfortable and wanted to move from chair to chair. Mom was not in the best shape since her stroke and her heart has a fibrillation, but she continued to walk around the house and helped him get seated from chair to chair because he was the love of her life. The last few days he had been missing the chair when he sat and would fall to the ground, never breaking a bone, thank God. This morning he missed the chair landed on my Mom's feet made a gurgling sound and became still. My mother untangled herself from my father and their canes, found a phone and called 911. The emergency vehicles were there in ten minutes. They carried my father out of the house on a stretcher and were truly compassionate to my mother.

The doctor came into the waiting room while Mom was telling me this story and explained a few things to us. About fifteen minutes after he fell, my father received an epinephrine injection in the ambulance and his heart began beating again. Then his heart stopped a second time and they administered another injection. The doctor said Dad was very ill. His heart was maintaining just a five percent function and had not been pumping for over 15 minutes meaning for that length of time there was no blood flow to the brain. He most likely would have brain damage if by some miracle his weak heart could keep him alive.

Mom and I went into Dad's ICU room first to see him. I held his hand and prayed with him and for him. I had to keep strong for Mom. Mom cried and I held her as the machines beeped, frantically trying to keep Dad alive. Technicians came into the room to x-ray Dad's chest and Mom and I were asked to step out of the room into the hallway to wait. Mom and I looked at each other and we knew Dad would not be with us much longer. We understood that the fact he was alive at all was amazing.

I did not feel Dad's presence while I was with him in his room, but I felt him with Mom and me in the hospital hallway. I felt his concern for my Mom, but most of all I felt a beautiful love and sweet peace. Just like the love he showed me when I was a little girl. I sensed that unconditional love I felt when we would dance together in the kitchen and I was on his shoes or when he would carry me to bed and toss me on my blanket and tell me "sweet dreams." I knew he was there and that he had always loved me and after being so sick for so long was now ready to go home to be with our Father in heaven.

After the X-rays were completed we were allowed back into the room. As Mom and I stood there quietly deep in thought, watching him, the alarms went off and additional hospital staff ran into Dad's room. They began removing large quantities of fluid from around his lungs through his mouth. Dad was drowning in his own body fluid. They were able to stabilize Dad. I looked at Mom and I knew she needed rest. I needed rest also, but I don't have the health issues she does. One of my brothers took her home so she could have a much-needed break. I went home too with the plan to pick her up in two hours to see Dad again before night time. The doctor said in cases like Dad's their hearts usually fail during the night.

We were home for about an hour when the hospital called my mom to tell us Dad was passing. We all rushed up to the ICU, but Dad passed before our return. We all went to his room. I knelt by his bed and prayed and thanked him for loving me unconditionally. Everyone said their goodbyes. As we left the room a Christian chaplain asked if we would like to go back to the room with him and say prayers for my father. My family returned to the peaceful room where my father's body rested to pray for the repose of my dad's soul. All the machines were gone. I put my hand on Dad as my family held hands together and said the Lord's Prayer. My mother commented that praying with us, with Dad, brought her peace. I am very glad that the reverend came when he did; it was not a coincidence.

We had a mass at church for my Dad. Mom did not want a wake at a funeral home. It would be too exhausting for her. We agreed to keep Mom as healthy as we could for as long as we could. The church filled with family and friends. Some believed in God, some in the Trinity, and some felt compelled to come to my church because they loved my dad, my mom, my family, or because they loved me. That church was bursting with people who came out of love. I felt a beautiful energy and I knew my dad was watching his sons and my husband carry his urn in an urn arc up to the altar. I knew he listened and watched my brother, his oldest son, as he spoke about Dad's life and the blessings we were a part of. Then my son, Dad's youngest grandson, read from the Bible. We celebrated Dad's life in God's name, recognizing that every life is a miracle and every day is a gift.

Chapter 17
Faith and Hope

Angel and her pup

Angel was always ready to learn something new. As her training progressed, she received a new trainer or two and her weight continued to increase. My friends and I would comment on how Angel must have eaten some watermelon seeds, because it looked like there was a large watermelon in her stomach. At times, she was having some difficulty moving on land because of her increasing girth. I would smile at her as I watched her attempt to be the graceful sea lion she was a few months ago.

One day in May, I asked Angel to present her flipper to me during a training session. She was about to lift her flipper for me to examine when she stopped. Her attention went to her abdomen. She looked at her stomach and opened her mouth. I smiled to myself and asked her again for her flipper; she looked at me and then held her flipper up. I gave her a fish and told her she was a good girl. Then I asked her to lie down. She did as I requested, then slowly turned and looked at her tail and again opened her mouth. She always let me know when she was uncomfortable or scared by opening her mouth. This was no exception.

On June 5, 2017, she hopped on the scale during her morning feeding—the scale read 246 pounds. Angel weighed 199 pounds in December. She had gained 47 pounds. California sea lion pups weigh on average 16 pounds when they are born. I was certain she was about to give birth very soon, but with that weight I was truly concerned about how large the pup would be and the difficulty she would have delivering it. Then, once the pup began its swimming lessons with Angel, I was concerned about how she was going to get it out of the water. To this day she has not used her mouth for retrieving toys. She has always used her flippers or her nose to push things to me. Remember, she is the survivor of bullet wounds to her flipper. This handicap could impair her ability to pull the pup from the water.

On June 6, 2017, her appetite decreased. She would hop out of the water at times and eat a fish, but then slowly go back into the outside pool. Her routine for years has been to enter the inside holding area at every feeding. This was not happening. For the pup's safety and to monitor their health more effectively, we were hoping to lock her inside the rooms she was accustomed to before the pup's birth.

The next morning, I found Angel had gone inside on her own accord to the doorway between the ISO room and main room. This was the same place she gave birth to her stillborn pup a year ago. It astonished me and I was very grateful that out of all the places Angel could give birth she chose a spot directly in front of the only windows where we could observe her when she was inside. Since she came to our zoo as an injured, rehabilitated pup six and a half years ago, we always entered the holding area through this same door. Some may say it was a coincidence, but I know she wanted us near her. She had too many choices for this to be accidental.

Every Day Is a Gift

We recognized labor had begun because we could see her abdomen tighten then relax. She pulled herself to the inside pool and swam erratically. She went back on land to strain and flex her rear flippers. Our video cameras clocked the time she entered the holding area at 3:30 a. m. It was now 8:40 a. m. We watched and I prayed. In my heart, I asked God for His mercy. At 10:00 a. m., I left the sea lion area to take care of the hyena and wolves. I needed to be busy; watching her was not helping anyone. At 10:30 I received a radio call to come back to the sea lion area. I headed back quickly. When I glanced into the holding room window, I saw her labor had intensified. She was vocalizing when normally she is a very quiet animal. She went around in circles on land for several minutes then her water broke. Soon after, we saw the back flippers of the pup emerging from Angel. The pup was in a breach position. Someone suggested I call another sea lion expert and consult with her about what Angel was going through. I told the expert about Angel's stillbirth last year and that this labor was proving to be difficult. She said that first-born sea lions are often stillborn. These pups are usually small female pups. Angel's first pup was small, just fourteen pounds and female. She also told me the second pup of these mothers are very often large male pups and are delivered breach. The labor could be hours and she assured me that everything would be "Okay."

I ran into the kitchen and conveyed this information to my colleagues who were watching Angel on the monitor. The information appeared to make everyone feel better; we wanted the pup to make a healthy entrance. We were holding our breaths and were quietly in our own thoughts, not knowing what to expect. At 12:17 p. m. Angel gave that final push and the pup was born. She cared for this pup as she had her first pup. We watched as she cleared out its mouth with her mouth. She rolled it with her flippers on the floor of the holding room and tended to it. Because

134

she was behind a door when she gave birth, we only caught glimpses of these actions.

In my heart I began to pray, "Dear Lord, whatever your will is, I understand," but before I could complete that prayer, I began pleading to my Lord, "Oh please, please, please let it be alive, please, for Angel, please."

We squinted through the windows which now were covered by many smeared human nose prints. Someone said they thought they saw the pup move. It looked to me as if the pup might have been moving because Angel was moving it while cleaning it. Then one of the pup's flippers moved and someone said, "LOOK, IT IS BREATHING!" Tears began running down my cheeks like they are now while I am writing this and remembering. The pup made little noises and Angel responded. They began to bond. Truly, every day is a gift! Angel's humans hugged each other and we allowed ourselves to be happy and hopeful once again.

Epilogue

Shortly after Star's death, I was listening to a Christian radio station, when a woman called in and what she said really moved me. She said that when something horrible happens to her, she can't wait to see the beautiful things God is going to make out of it. She has great faith. I am trying to look at life like the lady on the radio station; I cannot wait to see the good God is going to make out of the loss of my father, Star, Hut, and Sunny. I dig deep into my heart and open my eyes wide and look. All I can do is have faith, pray often, and love. I knew Star could not come back. She was in heaven with Our Lord along with my dad, Puff, Flounder, Hut, Sunny, Angel's stillborn pup, and all of God's creatures that He has called back home. We don't know too much about heaven, but enough to know it is where God's kingdom is. God's kingdom is paradise. In my paradise, there are animals. He did create animals before humans and all that is good is God and He is love. Imagine that kingdom! God loves us so much. We only need to love Him back. In the New Testament of the Bible it says the only way we may enter heaven is through God's son, our Savior, Jesus Christ. This is what I believe. I hope I will see you someday in God's glory. Look me up! I will be the soul that is praising our Lord while singing, dancing, hugging and kissing and perhaps playing fetch with some much-loved sea lions.

If you could only see the sea lions' garden—in the back of their habitat, you would see a red rose for Flounder that blossoms every summer. You will notice a beautiful group of purple flowers in the back right that bloom in the spring and are beautiful all spring and summer reminding me of Hut and his gentle ways. I planted a little bunch of yellow mums close to the purple flowers to represent the sweet innocence of Sunny; she will be forever near Hut. In the front of the garden that blooms every October 4 is the largest bush of daisies I have ever seen. It grows larger and more beautiful each year. I planted it in 2012 for my sweet animal child, Puff. Not planted by me, is a flower that just grew fast and wild and is breath-taking, like my Starfish. These wild tiny daisies entwined with Puff's large daisies with no help from me. After she passed on September 15, I searched for the perfect flower to represent Star's personality. On September 20, I noticed this natural bouquet growing throughout the garden. When I saw this addition to my garden, I took a deep breath, closed my eyes, and thought to myself, "Star always knew what to do and now she sends me a message from heaven. "GOOD GIRL, STARFISH!" See you soon...

Acknowledgements

Thank you, Maureen Whalen, for your editing skills, devotion to me, and the animals. You are as patient as you are sweet! This book's beautiful cover was designed by Jenelle Penders of Jenelle Lynn Design. Thank you, Jenelle! Tim Ostrander, thank you for proof reading and approving this book for the nineteen-year-olds in the world; this was wonderful for me to hear! I love each one of you.

To all the people who loved Star, Angel, PJ, Sunny and Hut with me, from our staff, docents, volunteers and zoo guests, we were fortunate that we had these wonderful animals because they taught us about sea lion behavior and about the human-animal bond. Most importantly we learned to love more than we did before we met them. Zoo animals are loved very much by their zookeeper friends, and to some of us, are family. All creation should be cared for and loved. Thank you to the animals that have changed us into kinder human beings and thank you, God, for creating them.

A portion of the proceeds from the sale of this book will benefit the United States of America's troops and veterans. My father, Tom Blazynski, who passed away April 3, 2017, served in the United States Army. He taught me by example how to live the American dream, through hard work and loving one another. Dad worked three jobs at one time and was the father to many foster children after he adopted me and my brothers and sister. I love you, Dad!

A portion will also go to Catholic Family Center. My parents adopted me through this not-for-profit organization along with all my siblings. My husband and I adopted our two sons from there as well. All prospective parents should have a chance to be counseled on the choices that are available when they get pregnant. Every child deserves a chance to love and be loved. Now this book about love is in print and its sales will benefit others.

Because you have read this story, I hope Star, Sunny, Angel, PJ, and Hut are in your heart and not just a memory in this zookeeper's thoughts and prayers. Life is full of beauty and pain. It is up to us what we focus on, how we handle it, and what we do with it. I focus on the Lord and the beauty He created and gave me. I handled it by getting back up like my mother has so many times. Then I wrote this love story to share with the world. May God bless us all.

Every Day Is a Gift

About the Author

Mary Ellen Ostrander began working with zoo animals in 1985. She has two wonderful sons, four dogs, a cat, and three birds. She is a member of the International Marine Animal Trainers' Association (IMATA), the American Association of Zoo Keepers (AAZK), and the Animal Behavior Management Alliance (ABMA).

Made in the USA
Lexington, KY
21 November 2019